WITTGENSTEIN'S TRACTATUS

An Introduction

H. O. MOUNCE

The University of Chicago Press

The University of Chicago Press, Chicago 60637
Basil Blackwell Publisher, Oxford, England

Library of Congress Cataloging in Publication Data

Mounce, H. O.
  Wittgenstein's Tractatus.
  1. Wittgenstein, Ludwig, 1889–1951. Tractatus
logico-philosophicus. 2. Logic, Symbolic and
mathematical. 3. Languages – Philosophy. I. Title.
B3376.W563T7346   192   81-40474

ISBN 0-226-54321-8   AACR2

CONTENTS

ACKNOWLEDGEMENTS

The author and publisher are indebted to Routledge and Kegan Paul and Humanities Press Inc., New Jersey 07716, for permission to quote from Wittgenstein's *Tractatus Logico-Philosophicus* in the translation by D. F. Pears and B. F. McGuinness; to Routledge and Kegan Paul and Schocken Books Inc. for permission to quote from Rush Rhees' *Discussions of Wittgenstein*, copyright © 1970 by Rush Rhees; to Basil Blackwell Publisher for permission to quote from Friedrich Waismann's *Ludwig Wittgenstein and the Vienna Circle* and Wittgenstein's *Notebooks 1914–1916* and *Philosophical Grammar*; and to George Allen and Unwin for permission to quote from Bertrand Russell's *The Principles of Mathematics*.

PREFACE

The only purpose of this short book is to be useful to students who have trouble in finding their whereabouts in one of the most difficult of philosophical works. It seems to me that there is a need for such a book. There are a number of excellent commentaries on the market, but they are all, so far as I can see, more suited to the scholar than to the undergraduate, for whom they are often more difficult to follow than the *Tractatus* itself.

Since my aim in writing this book is simply to be useful rather than to produce a work of original scholarship, I have not hesitated to borrow from the writings of others. For example, in a part of my Introduction I have closely followed a chapter in A. Kenny's book on Wittgenstein.[1] This is because it has seemed to me idle to tamper with a job that Kenny has already done well. For the most part, I have not acknowledged these borrowings; indeed in many cases I should probably be unable to do so. After having studied the *Tractatus* over some twenty years I should be at a loss to determine on many a point whether it was mine or whether it was someone else's. I hope that anyone who recognizes a point as his own will remember the aim of the book and will be content to know that he has my gratitude.

There is, however, one debt that I am obliged to acknowledge. This is my debt to Rush Rhees,[2] who first taught me the *Tractatus* and whose interpretation, in its essentials, still seems to me the soundest available.

[1] *Wittgenstein* by A. Kenny (Allen Lane/The Penguin Press, London, 1973).

[2] Rush Rhees is the author of *Without Answers* and *Discussions of Wittgenstein* and is one of Wittgenstein's literary executors.

INTRODUCTION

Wittgenstein's *Tractatus Logico-Philosphicus*, as its full title makes clear, is a work in philosophical logic. To understand it, one has to consider some of the developments in logic that preceded it, and especially the developments that were brought about by Frege and Russell.[1] Frege, next to Aristotle, is the greatest name in formal logic, the study of valid inference, and his work had a great influence on Wittgenstein. So we must begin by reminding ourselves of his main achievements.

Frege's great achievement was to invent a symbolic system by which logicians could formulate both the types of inference studied by Aristotle and those to which Aristotle's methods cannot be applied.

> If it will rain this afternoon, the match will be cancelled.
> It will rain this afternoon.
> Therefore the match will be cancelled.

This is a valid inference but not one that is handled by Aristotle. This is because Aristotle's analysis depended on splitting the

[1] The most accessible works of Gottleb Frege (1848–1925) are *Die Grundlagen der Arithmetik* (1884) translated by J. L. Austin as *The Foundations of Arithmetic* and a selection from his articles entitled *Translations from the Philosophical Writings of Gottleb Frege* (1952) edited by P. Geach and M. Black.

Bertrand Russell (1872–1970) was the author of numerous works in philosophy, of which the most relevant to this book are *The Principles of Mathematics* (1903), *Principia Mathematica* (with A. N. Whitehead, 3 volumes 1910–13), and a collection of his essays entitled *Logic and Knowledge* (1956).

propositions contained in the inference into subjects and predicates:

All Greeks are Europeans.	All S is P
All Europeans are dark skinned.	All P is M
Therefore all Greeks are dark skinned.	∴ All S is M

Now the validity of the inference we are considering does not depend on the internal constitutions of the propositions involved. It depends rather on the relationships between the propositions taken as wholes. Thus it can be symbolized 'If p then q; and p; therefore q'. The way in which the proposition one substitutes for 'p', for example, splits up into subject and predicate, or whether it does so at all, is irrelevant. In Frege's logic, inferences of this kind are given a central place. They are handled by the use of two kinds of symbols, one kind standing for the propositions (p, q, r), the other for the connectives or, as they are called, constants such as 'if . . . then' which relate the propositions together. As we shall see, Wittgenstein has much to say in the *Tractatus* about the nature of these constants. In the *Tractatus* they are set out usually in Russell's notation, 'if . . . then' being represented by '⊃', 'either . . . or' by 'v' etc. The negation sign '~' would also be considered a constant.

But there arises here a further point that is of interest in studying the *Tractatus*. We have seen that the valid inference 'If it will rain this afternoon, the match will be cancelled; it will rain this afternoon; therefore the match will be cancelled' may be set out symbolically as 'If p then q; and p; therefore q'. Now some have expressed this by saying that 'If p then q; then q' expresses a logical truth that guarantees the validity of the inference 'If it rains this afternoon etc.' and any other inference of the same form. In other words, 'If it rains this afternoon etc.' is valid because it is an expression of the logical truth 'If p then q; and p; then q' and any other inference which is an expression of that truth, which can be written in that symbolic form, is necessarily valid also. Now Frege develops his calculus by concentrating on so-called logical truths of this kind, and setting them out in something like the form of a geometrical system. He takes a small number of such truths as axioms and, adopting the rule of inference 'Given *A* and "If *A* then *B*" infer *B*', he shows how one can derive from them an unlimited number of other logical truths. Russell and Whitehead, some years later, developed a comparable system based on a different set of axioms. Now some who have reflected on what is occurring in the development of these systems have found themselves puzzled in certain respects. They have been puzzled especially, for example, about the nature of logical truth. It seems to have about it a certain necessity which distinguishes it from the truth of the statements in, say, the physical sciences. But how is this necessity to be elucidated? Or again, consider the relationships between the logical truths and the axioms on which they are based. Do they depend for their truth on these axioms? If so, what do the axioms depend on for their truth? If not, in what sense are they derived from them? Again, consider the inference 'If it will rain this afternoon etc.'. We say this is valid because it is an expression of the logical truth 'If *p* then *q*; and *p*; then *q*'. But what is the nature of the 'because'? How precisely does the validity of the inference depend on the logical truth?

Now, at this stage, it is not necessary that we dwell on these questions; we shall do so, in some detail, later. The point is simply that they express a certain puzzlement about the nature of logic. They are questions which arise not so much when one is developing a logical system as when one reflects on what one is doing in so developing it. As such, they belong not to logic but to philosophy of logic. As we go along we shall encounter other questions of the same type and we shall see that it is precisely with questions of this type that Wittgenstein is concerned in the *Tractatus*. But first we need to look at some further aspects of Frege's work.

We have seen how Frege dealt with certain types of inference that had not been formalized by Aristotle. But in some ways his most remarkable achievement lay in his treatment of the types of inference that Aristotle had formalized. He did this by introducing a device from mathematics which is called a function. In algebra the expression '$x^2 + 1$' represents a function of the variable x. It is a function of x because its value will depend on what we substitute for x, for the variable. Substitute 2 for x and the value of the expression is 5; substitute 3 and the value is 10; and so on. The number we substitute for the variable x is known as the argument. Frege took this device and applied it to propositions. For example, take the proposition 'Caesar conquered Gaul'. Instead of speaking about 'Caesar' as the subject and 'conquered Gaul' as the predicate we can speak of 'x conquered Gaul' as the function to which 'Caesar' supplies the argument. In short, we treat the predicate by analogy with '$x^2 + 1$' and treat 'Caesar' by analogy with the number, say 2, that we substitute for x. As a matter of fact we have here a choice. For we could also treat 'Caesar conquered x' as the function to which 'Gaul' supplies the argument; or gain 'x conquered y' as the function to which the arguments are supplied by 'Caesar' and 'Gaul'.

But what here is the equivalent of the *value* of a function? The value of '$x^2 + 1$' for the argument 2 is a particular number 5. What is the value of the function 'x conquered Gaul' for the argument Caesar? Frege said that the value was either the True or the False. Or, to put that a different way, if one provides an argument for 'x conquered Gaul' one gets a proposition which is either true or false, in the technical phrase, has a truth value. Thus if the function 'x conquered Gaul' has the argument 'Caesar' it is true, if 'Mrs Thatcher', false.

Let us now see how this enables us to formalize Aristotelian inferences, to develop what is known as the predicate calculus. It is clear, to begin with, that these inferences cannot be fitted into the propositional calculus, because in that calculus propositions are symbolized only as wholes, i.e. they are symbolized without regard to the internal structure of the propositions on which the validity of the inferences depends. Thus, 'All Greeks are bald; Socrates is a Greek; therefore Socrates is bald' will be symbolized as '*p, q*; therefore *r*'. But '*p, q*; therefore *r*' will fit an invalid as well as a valid inference – for example, 'All men are mortal; Sandy is a dog; therefore the moon is green'. How then are we to proceed? The first step is to realize that a statement such as 'All Greeks are bald' is equivalent to the statement 'If anyone is a Greek then he is bald'. The single propositions can be written as two propositions connected by 'if. . . then'. Let us now write each of the two propositions so connected in the form of a function — 'If *x* is Greek then *x* is bald'. When written in this way, the proposition 'All Greeks are bald' falls within the scope of Frege's system. Or rather it almost does so. There is one ambiguity to clear up. 'If *x* is Greek then *x* is bald' can be misleading because it is ambiguous between some particular *x* and any *x*. We want the 'any *x*'; we want to capture the generality of '*All* Greeks are bald'. We must therefore take steps to write in this generality. Thus instead of 'If *x* is Greek then *x* is bald', we write 'For all *x*, if *x* is Greek then *x* is bald'. What we now have is a sentence roughly equivalent to 'Take whatever you like: if it is Greek, it is bald'. If we reflect on what we are saying when we say 'All Greeks are bald', we shall see that the rough equivalence holds. In much the same way, if we want to represent '*Some* Greeks are bald' we write 'For some *x*, *x* is Greek and *x* is bald', which is roughly equivalent to 'There is something which is both Greek and bald'. The two expressions fully formalized would run '$(x)\ (Gx \supset Bx)$' and '$(\exists x)\ Gx \cdot Bx$'. With this equipment we are able to bring Aristotelian inferences within our system.

Here then in the briefest of outlines we have the elements of Frege's symbolic system. We need to have a grasp of this, first, because a knowledge of this system, or at least others closely allied to it, is presupposed in the *Tractatus* and, second, because it is through reflecting on this system that we can come to see some of the philosophical problems that the *Tractatus* was written to deal with. We have already illustrated this latter point; let us now do so in more detail.

Frege was led to develop his symbolic system initially through a concern for mathematics. His aim had been to show that mathematics was an extension of logic. Russell, working at first independently of Frege, had the same aim. In the course of his work Russell came upon acute problems that were philosophical in nature, problems that seemed to put in question, so far as he and Frege were concerned, the very nature of logic. These problems can be illustrated very easily by reference to a paradox which has long been known in philosophy. Take the assertion, made by a Cretan, that all Cretans are liars. If he is telling the truth, his statement is false; for he is a Cretan and, *ex hypothesi*, truthful. In order to tell the truth, he would have to be lying. So set out, the paradox may seem just a trick. But it can give rise to serious perplexity. Let us put the matter in a slightly different way. It seems clear that certain statements can be used to refer to themselves. For example, 'This statement contains five words' can be taken to refer to itself and when so taken can be seen to be true. Now consider 'This statement is false'. If taken to refer to itself is it true or false? Well, if we assume first that it is false, then since it says that it is false we have to conclude also that it is true. On the othert hand if we assume that it is true, we have to conclude also that it is false, for it says that it is false and, on this assumption, says so truly. Thus the statement, when taken to refer to itself, presents us with a contradiction. But why is this more than a trivial trick? The reason is that the statement seems to have been constructed quite logically. The words are ordinary ones, evidently meaningful, and the procedure of self reference seems in other cases to work well enough. How is it that logical procedures can issue in a contradiction? Can it be that there is some contradiction in logic itself?

This paradox, though akin to, is not quite the same as

Russell's. To see how Russell's paradox arises we need to understand in more detail what he was hoping to achieve in *Principia Mathematica*. His aim was to show that mathematics was founded on logic, was, in short, thoroughly logical. In order to do so, he needed to show that the notion of number could be derived from notions that were not themselves arithmetical but which belonged solely to pure logic; and he thought he could succeed in doing this by defining number in terms of the notion of a class. More precisely, he defined numbers as classes of classes. The number 2 he defined as the class of pairs, number 3 as the class of trios, etc. This may seem on the face of it entirely circular, as if one were to define the number 2 as the class of all classes with two members. Russell, however, had a way of avoiding this circularity which for our present purpose we can take for granted. The point, for our purpose, is that in developing this idea he came upon a contradiction. To see the paradox, one has to remember, first, that it is essential to Russell's procedure that classes can be classified. One must be able to speak of classes of classes, and indeed of classes of classes of classes. Classes in short must be capable of being members of other classes. This may raise the question of whether a class can be a member of itself. Thus the class of chairs is not a chair, but the class of all classes is itself a class. It seems we can distinguish between classes that are members of themselves and those that are not. Now we get our paradox. Take the class of classes that are not members of themselves. Is that a member of itself? If it is then necessarily it is not a member of itself; if it is not a member of itself then necessarily it is. We have a paradox very like the paradox of the liar.

Russell treated this as a very serious matter. For if number is to be defined in terms of classes and if this notion leads to a contradiction then it seems there must be some contradiction in number, in arithmetic, itself. To try and overcome these difficulties Russell introduced his theory of types. He argued that a statement such as 'The class of all chairs is not a chair' so far from being true is really meaningless because it predicates of a logical type what does not belong to it. One can say of an object that it is not a chair, but not of a class of objects; and similarly what one can say of a class of objects one cannot say of a class of a class of objects. In this way, Russell hoped to prevent the paradox of classes from arising.

There is one further matter we must consider before turning to the *Tractatus* itself. In attempting to show that number can be understood in terms of classes, Russell made a particular assumption which seems on the face of it to be empirical, to depend on how the world happens to be. This assumption may not be evident if we confine ourselves to low numbers. Thus when Russell defines 2 as the class of pairs it never occurs to us to wonder if there is such a class, for it is evident that pairs of things exist. But it is a feature of the number series that it can be extended indefinitely. Now suppose there are a finite number of things in the universe. Suppose, for the sake of the argument, that there are one million things. Then there is no class of things with more than a million members. But in that case, how can we count beyond a million? Exactly the same point holds however many things there are in the universe, so long as the universe is finite. For however many there are we shall always be capable of counting beyond them. To cover this, Russell made the assumption that the number of objects in the universe is infinite. This is the so-called axiom of infinity.

Wittgenstein was profoundly dissatisfied with this axiom. At 5.551 in the *Tractatus*, he says, 'Our fundamental principle is that whenever a question can be decided by logic at all it must be possible to decide it without more ado. (And if we get into a position where we have to look at the world for an answer to such a problem, that shows that we are on a completely wrong track.)' Now Russell in his analysis of number is forced to look at the world, or at least to make assumptions about it. Thus he cannot complete his analysis unless he assumes that the number of objects in the universe is infinite. Now Wittgenstein's objection, it is important to note, is not that Russell might be mistaken in his assumption. Rather, his objection is that there is something wrong with Russell's analysis if he is forced to make an assumption, right or wrong, of this kind. For suppose he is right in his assumption. Still it must in a sense be an accidental matter that he is right. Or, to put that differently, his assumption will be empirical and not logical. But, for Wittgenstein, there was an absolute distinction between the empirical and the logical, such that the latter would never depend on the former.

This point provides us with the best entry into the *Tractatus*. We shall best get to the heart of the work by seeing why, for Wittgenstein, the empirical or contingent on the one hand and the logical or necessary on the other have to be distinguished sharply from one another. Wittgenstein stresses this point in a variety of ways throughout the *Tractatus*. Here, for example, is a cluster of quotations from pages 62–3 of the Pears–McGuinness translation:[2]

6.1222 . . . Not only must a proposition of logic be irrefutable by any possible experience, but it must also be unconfirmable by any possible experience.

6.1231 The mark of a logical proposition is *not* general validity.

To be general means no more than to be accidentally valid for all things. . . .

6.1232 The general validity of logic might be called essential, in contrast with the accidental general validity of such propositions as 'All men are mortal'. . . .

Let us take this last proposition 'All men are mortal'. This is true because it happens to be true of each man that he dies, and

---

[2] First paperback edition, with revised translation, 1974. This translation, by D. F. Pears and B. F. McGuinness, was first published by Routledge & Kegan Paul, London, 1961. The *Tractatus* was first published in Germany in 1921, and the first English translation, by C. K. Ogden, was published in 1922.

we believe it because all the men of whom we have heard or have had experience have died. Compare this with the proposition 'All unmarried men are bachelors'. Is this true because it happens to be true of each unmarried man that he is a bachelor? Have we gradually become convinced through finding in case after case that an unmarried man is a bachelor, that all unmarried men are bachelors? This would be an odd way of describing the matter.[3] Our certainty that all unmarried men are bachelors manifestly does not depend on the weight of empirical evidence. We are no more certain after a million cases than we were to begin with. There is, we might say, an internal or necessary relation between being an unmarried man and being a bachelor. In this, it is to be contrasted with being a Welshman and being over six feet in height, which is external and accidental. It may be so; but it is not necessarily so. Indeed it is not necessarily so even if it is true in every case. Even if during a given generation every Welshman turned out to be over six feet, the relation would still not be an internal one. Its truth would still depend on its happening to be true of each Welshman and so would not be a proposition we could determine in advance of the empirical evidence.

The logical, then, is to be distinguished from the empirical. This does not mean, we shall see, that there is no connection between logic and the facts, between logic and the world. But the necessity of a logical inference, or of a so-called logical truth, does not depend on what *happens* to be so in the world. Yet this point once grasped may itself lead one astray. One may, for example, be tempted to suppose that if a logical truth does not depend on what is so in the empirical world it must depend on what is so in some world other than the empirical. Frege, for

---

[3] I am aware that there are some philosophers who would not find it an odd way of describing the matter. These philosophers seem to me confused. But to discuss their view in a work devoted to exposition would, in any case, be irrelevant.

example, gave an analysis of arithmetical propositions, according to which their truth depended on their corresponding to what he called abstract objects. Thus '2 + 2 = 4', he was clear, is not made true by something to which it corresponds in the empirical world. But how could it be true at all unless there were something, some set of objects, of some kind to which it corresponds? A similar view might be held of the propositions of logic. Take the proposition '$p \supset q$; and p; then q'; or again '$p \vee q$; and $\sim q$; then p'. These propositions are necessarily true and their truth does not depend on what happens to hold in the empirical world. The content of 'p' and 'q' in these propositions, for example, is irrelevant. They will be true whatever the content of 'p' and 'q', their truth plainly depending on the so-called logical constants ' $\supset$ ', '$\vee$' and '$\sim$'. But then, it may be said, these constants must surely represent some objects. For if they represent nothing, how can propositions containing them be true? Russell, as well as Frege, held views of this kind, as one can see from the following passage in which he is discussing what he calls 'the indefinables', i.e. the fundamental notions of logic, of which the logical constants, or his own notion of a class, would be examples.

> The discussion of indefinables – which forms the chief part of philosophical logic – is the endeavour to see clearly, and to make others see clearly, the entities concerned, in order that the mind may have that kind of acquaintance with them which it has with redness or the taste of a pineapple. Where, as in the present case, the indefinables are obtained primarily as the necessary residue in a process of analysis, it is often easier to know that there must be such entities than actually to perceive them; there is a process analogous to that which resulted in the discovery of Neptune, with the difference that the final stage – the search with a mental telescope for the entity that has been inferred – is often the most difficult part of the undertaking. In the case of classes, I must confess, I have failed to perceive any concept fulfilling the conditions requisite for the notion of *class*. And the contradiction dis-

cussed in Chapter **X** proves that something is amiss, but what it is
I have hitherto failed to discover.[4]

Notice that Russell here treats the notion of class as if it stood
for some object or entity comparable with the objects of
astronomy. He is clear, of course, that the object or entity is not
an empirical object. As he says, we look for it not with a
physical but with a mental telescope. Nevertheless classes, and
the logical constants, do stand for objects of some kind. For
Wittgenstein, however, this was no better than the view that
logic represents empirical objects. On Wittgenstein's view,
logic simply does not represent objects, whether they be of an
empirical or of a quasi-empirical kind. The distinction, in short,
between the logical and the empirical is a radical one. Or to put
this in another way, logic is radically different from any of the
other sciences. It is not as if the physical sciences tell us about the
physical world and logic about a non-physical one. That is not
to make the difference radical enough. For Wittgenstein, logic
does not tell us or make statements about anything at all.

'My fundamental idea' says Wittgenstein at 4.0312, 'is that the
"logical constants" are not representatives; that there can be no
representatives of the *logic* of the facts.' Thus the logical truth
'$p \vee q$; and $\sim q$; then p' is not true because it corresponds to a set
of objects, or set of facts. All correspondence lacks the hardness
of logical necessity; it is merely accidental. This is not to say that
logic reflects nothing of the world. But it reflects, on
Wittgenstein's view, by showing not by saying. This indeed is
the central doctrine of the *Tractatus*. Logic differs from all the
other sciences because the other sciences say something about
the world whereas logic only shows something. At 4.022
Wittgenstein says, 'A proposition *shows* its sense. A proposition
shows how things stand *if* it is true. And it *says that* they do so
stand.' And at 4.1212, 'What *can* be shown, *cannot* be said.'

[4] *The Principles of Mathematics* (2nd edn, Allen and Unwin, London, 1937),
page xv.

To illustrate this point, consider the proposition 'It is raining'. This says something about the world because it has a logical structure, because it has sense; but it shows its sense in your being able to grasp what it says about the world, not in what it says about its sense. Logic, in short, is not what statements talk about; it is what enables them to talk about something else, namely, the world or the facts. Russell, therefore, in speaking of the propositions of logic as if they represented objects is misconceiving the nature of logic itself. For logic is not something which is represented; it is what makes representation possible.[5] As such, though it cannot be represented itself, it shows itself in that there are things that *can* be represented.

As we shall see later in detail, Wittgenstein illustrated these points by comparing a proposition with a picture. A man knows what a picture is about, say a painting of a wheatfield, not because the picture tells him, but because he can see from the picture what it is about. He can see this, as it were, *in* the picture even if what it pictures, the wheatfield, has never existed. Of course, what the picture is about can also be put into words. But Wittgenstein's point would be that when we say what the picture is about then what we are really doing is introducing another picture. The statement stands to the picture as, in another context, a picture might stand to a statement. For example, suppose someone cannot get across to you what he means and finally he draws it on a sheet of paper. Wittgenstein's point would be that this is possible because what we have are just two different kinds of pictures; the statement is a kind of picture, too. In other words, the sense of picture *A* can be elucidated by means of *B*, an equivalent picture. But what one cannot do is represent the sense of picture *A* (say what it says) in the way that picture *A* can represent a state of affairs holding in the world. The sense of a proposition is not something that corresponds to it in the way that a set of objects or facts may be said

[5] It would have been better, though perhaps at this stage confusing, to say that logic *is* the possibility of representation.

so to correspond. This point can in fact be illustrated by another, related, point. For while you can bring out the meaning of one picture by showing a person another, this only works if you do not have to explain what the other picture is about. At some point, in short, you have to rely on a person's grasping the sense of what is said without having it explained to him. Sense can only be shown; it cannot be stated.

This, again, is why logic must differ radically from any other science. Logic cannot explain what logical structure, or the sense of language, is in anything like the way that science explains the facts. For an understanding of logical structure or sense would be presupposed in giving the explanation. The explanation could be given, in other words, only to someone who already understood the logical structure or sense of language. Any theory in logic would therefore presuppose what it is seeking to explain.

Finally, these points need to be borne in mind when one reflects on what has been said about formal logic, the development of a logical calculus. Some philosophers have thought that formal logic reveals the principles or laws on which the logic of our language is founded, as if these principles would explain why, say, an argument in ordinary language was valid. This is a view that students sometimes hold when they first study formal logic. Formal logic, they sometimes think, will teach them how to reason. But it is evident, on reflection, that if they do not already know how to reason they will never understand formal logic. In short, we can develop a formal calculus only because we already have a grasp of validity. Wittgenstein was expressing these points when he said at 6.123 'Clearly the laws of logic cannot in their turn be subject to laws of logic'. What he thought, at the time of the *Tractatus*, was that a formal calculus would be useful in *showing* the logic already inherent in ordinary language. The logic of ordinary language, Wittgenstein held, is perfectly in order as it is. A language cannot be imperfectly logical. A thing either makes sense or it does not; there can be no mid-way position. What he believed, however, was that in ordinary language logical relations are not as evident to formal study as they might be in a calculus that was constructed especially to *display* those relations. Grammar, in ordinary language, often hides logical form. The use of a logical calculus, Wittgenstein thought, was to *show* the logic of ordinary language more clearly than ordinary language did itself. As we shall see, he thought that the formal systems developed by Frege and Russell fell short of this ideal in a number of ways.

CHAPTER 1

FACT AND THING

So far we have been picking out some of the central ideas in the *Tractatus*. Let us now turn to a systematic study of the text itself. In considering the details of the text, it will be important to keep in mind the central ideas that have already been outlined – for example, the idea that the logical constants do not represent and, going with it, the idea that logic belongs to what is shown and not to what is said. We shall see that Wittgenstein works towards these ideas from a number of directions and does so in prolific and ingenious detail. This indeed affords one of the pleasures of the *Tractatus*. Like the works of the great metaphysical philosophers, the *Ethics* of Spinoza, for example, it has about it something of the beauty of a mathematical construction.

The *Tractatus* is laid out according to a system of decimal numbers that Wittgenstein explains on the first page. Proposition 1.1 is a comment on proposition 1; proposition 1.11 is a comment on 1.1; and so on. Let us consider the propositions under 1.

1. The world is all that is the case.

   1.1 The world is the totality of facts, not of things.

   1.11 The world is determined by the facts, and by their being *all* the facts.

   1.12 For the totality of facts determines what is the case, and also whatever is not the case.

   1.13 The facts in logical space are the world.

1.2   The world divides into facts.

1.21   Each item can be the case or not the case while everything else remains the same.

The first proposition is elucidated by the second. But to understand the second, one needs to understand why Wittgenstein wishes to distinguish between facts and things. What precisely is the difference? To see this, it will be useful to consider propositions 1.13 and 1.21, taking the latter first. 'Each item can be the case or not the case while everything else remains the same.' This might strike some people as a denial of determinism. What is the case is quite undetermined by something else's being the case. But this is not at all what Wittgenstein means. What he means is that something's being the case is not determined by something else's being the case *as a matter of logic*. The sense in which things necessarily occur is not that of logical necessity. This indeed is another way of saying that logic does not determine what is the case. Nevertheless there is a connection between logic and the facts because, as Wittgenstein says at 1.13, it is the facts in logical space which constitute the world. But what is logical space? To understand this is also to understand why the world is the totality of facts, not of things.

Let us consider propositions 2–2.012:

2.   What is the case – a fact – is the existence of states of affairs.

2.01   A state of affairs (a state of things) is a combination of objects (things).

2.011   It is essential to things that they should be possible constituents of states of affairs.

2.012   In logic nothing is accidental: if a thing *can* occur in a state of affairs, the possibility of the state of affairs must be written into the thing itself.

To illustrate this, consider the propositions 'Socrates is fat' and 'Plato is thin'. These, we shall suppose, represent states of affairs. These states of affairs hold in the world; but notice that they

might not have done so. Socrates might have been thin and
Plato fat. Now what this shows is that states of affairs are
complex. For we can imagine them rearranged, the elements
appearing in combinations different from those in which they
actually appear. But in logic, says Wittgenstein at 2.012,
nothing is accidental; if a thing *can* occur in a state of affairs, the
possibility of the state of affairs must be written into the thing
itself. Thus it is written into Socrates and into Plato that each
can be fat and thin. There is a range of possible state of affairs
into which Socrates and Plato fit. Which of these state of affairs
are actual is not a matter of logic; but it is a matter of logic
which states of affairs are *possible*. Whether Socrates is fat or thin
is a matter of fact, but it is a matter of logic that he can be either
one or the other.

One may be reminded here of Frege's notion of a function.
Frege would analyse 'Socrates is fat' into a function 'x is fat' for
which 'Socrates' supplies the argument. One might put it by
saying that 'Socrates' fits the function 'x is fat'. Now this in a
way expresses what Wittgenstein has in mind when he says 'The
world is the totality of facts, not of things.' To say that the
world is a totality of things would be to leave out that things fit
together. Things exist only in facts. Moreover which facts a

thing *can* fit into is predetermined; it is written into the nature of
the thing. That is why it is not things but facts, and not just facts
but *facts in logical space*, that constitute the world. At 2.0131,
Wittgenstein gives further examples of logical space or logical
form. 'A speck in the visual field, though it need not be red,
must have some colour: it is, so to speak, surrounded by colour-
space. Notes must have *some* pitch, objects of the sense of touch
some degree of hardness, and so on.' Logical form shows itself in
that a speck must have some colour, a note some pitch, whereas
a speck cannot have a pitch, nor a note a colour. Specks fit with
colours, notes with pitches.

But there is a point here of great importance. It is important
not to think of logical space or form as a special kind of fact,

some kind of universal cement that holds things together. Consider again 'Socrates is fat'. 'x is fat' is the function into which the argument, 'Socrates', fits. Now suppose someone were to ask 'What makes it fit?' One might be tempted to reply 'Logical form'. But this would be very misleading, because it would suggest that logical form is some extra fact binding things together. Logical form, however, cannot be stated in this way. Rather, it shows itself *in* things fitting together. We must remember that logic does not determine any fact, but only what combinations are possible. What shows logical form is that 'Socrates is fat' is a possible combination, whereas 'Fatness is Socrates', for example, is not. Wittgenstein expresses this point at 2.03 by means of a brilliant image: 'In a state of affairs objects fit into one another like links in a chain.' A state of affairs, like a chain, is not just a collection, but a collection that holds together in a determinate way. But what holds together the links of a chain? Nothing, except their fitting into one another. Their fitting into one another is how they hold together. The same point applies to the combination of objects in a state of affairs. That they hold together in a determinate way shows something about their logical form. But logical form is not a further fact about them, that which holds them together.

The world, then, is the totality of facts in logical space; or, again, it is the totality of states of affairs, which are made up of objects fitting together in a determinate way. These are the conclusions of the first few pages of the *Tractatus*. But what kind of conclusions are they? They are statements about the world but, as we shall see later, they are not in any natural sense empirical propositions. They are statements about how the world has to be if there is to be sense, if there are to be propositions. We shall see this more clearly if we look closely for a moment at Wittgenstein's notion of an object. So far we have treated 'Socrates' as if it was the name of an object. This will do for the purpose of a first, rough, exposition. But it needs to be qualified. Neither persons nor indeed the physical objects of ordinary

experience will serve as objects in Wittgenstein's sense. Thus at
2.02 Wittgenstein says 'Objects are simple.' The objects of
ordinary experience are complex. A chair, for example, consists
of a back, a seat and legs. So, to grasp the name 'chair' one must
first understand, it would seem, the simpler names 'back', 'seat',
'legs'. Moreover these simpler names are not themselves simple.
They, too, can be further described and therefore depend for
their sense on names which are simpler still. The objects of
which Wittgenstein speaks, however, are absolutely simple.
The names for these objects can be grasped immediately for to
do so does not depend on grasping names that are simpler still.
What then would be an example of such objects? Wittgenstein
was never able to provide such an example. At the time of the
Tractatus, Wittgenstein believed that we could be sure that such
objects exist but that we cannot say what they are. This might
strike some as suspicious and Wittgenstein himself later came to
believe that this whole notion of simple objects was radically
confused. Why then was he inclined to speak of them in the
Tractatus? Because he felt that they were a requirement of
language. We can see what he had in mind if we go back for a
moment to our example of 'chair'. In order to grasp the
meaning of 'chair', we said, one has to grasp the meaning of
simpler words such as 'leg', 'seat', etc. But now this surely is not
a process that can go on for ever. If there are not some words
that stand directly for objects we shall never grasp a name at all.
At some point there must be objects, and therefore names,
which are absolutely simple. Otherwise there would be no
contact between language and the world and nothing could be
said. This is what Wittgenstein has in mind at 2.0211 where he
says that if there were no simple objects then whether a proposition had sense would depend on whether another proposition
was true. What he means is that if we could not be sure that
words stood for objects, we could never understand a given
proposition until we had another proposition which assured us
that the names of the first really did stand for objects. But this is

an impossible state of affairs. For whether a proposition has sense cannot be a contingent matter. What is contingent is whether it is true (or false). But in order to be true (or false) a proposition must *already* possess a sense. The sense of a proposition, in short, must be independent of whether it is in fact true or false. Consequently, there must be a contact between language and the world which is prior to the truth or falsity of what we say. Such a contact is to be found in the relationship between a simple name and a simple object, the relationship being such that the name just stands for the object independently of description.

What Wittgenstein is suggesting, then, is that the nature of language can be understood only if we understand also that the world is not simply a collection of things but is a totality of states of affairs which are made up of objects fitting together in a determinate way.[1] But how then is language related to the world? Wittgenstein suggests that the propositions of language picture or represent the world; and it is this famous comparison between a proposition and a picture that we must now consider in great detail.

[1] This is not an altogether happy way of putting the matter. But, as we shall see later, there is no altogether happy way of putting the matter. There is, in short, a pervasive difficulty, later to be discussed, about the nature of the statements that Wittgenstein makes, here and elsewhere, in the *Tractatus*.

CHAPTER 2

THE PROPOSITION
AS PICTURE

Wittgenstein introduces his comparison between a proposition and a picture at 2.1.

2.1   We picture facts to ourselves.

2.11   A picture represents a situation in logical space, the existence and non-existence of states of affairs.

2.12   A picture is a model of reality.

2.13   In a picture objects have the elements of the picture corresponding to them.

2.131   In a picture the elements of the picture are the representatives of the objects.

2.14   What constitutes a picture is that its elements are related to one another in a determinate way.

2.141   A picture is a fact.

2.15   The fact that the elements of a picture are related to one another in a determinate way represents that things are related to one another in the same way. . . .

At first sight these propositions may not seem difficult to understand. A proposition is like a picture because it represents something in the world and it does so because it is made of elements each of which stands for something in the world. In 'the book is on the table', for example, the words, 'the book' and 'the table' each stand for an object, the word 'on' stands for a relationship and the words when brought together on the page represent a particular arrangement of these objects, i.e. a state of affairs. Arrange the words differently and a different state of affairs is represented. Thus 'the book is on the table' represents one state of affairs; 'the table is on the book' represents quite another.

This is correct so far as it goes, but there is much that it omits, including in a sense the main point of Wittgenstein's comparison. To see this, let us consider the relation between the proposition 'the book is on the table' and the names that comprise it. The proposition as a whole has a sense because the names that comprise it stand for objects. At the time of the *Tractatus*, Wittgenstein identified the meaning of a name *with* the object for what it stood, so that the meaning of a name is, as it were, external to it, something for which it stands. But is the meaning of the proposition as a whole something for which it stands? At first sight, one may be inclined to suppose it is. Just as one can point to an actual book or table as the meaning of the words 'the book' or 'the table' so one can point to an actual state of affairs, in which the book is on the table, as what is represented by the proposition as a whole. But what if there is no such state of affairs. A moment's reflection will reveal that if the proposition is false there will be nothing to which it will even be plausible to point as what the proposition as a whole stands for. But a proposition has the same sense whether or not it is false. As we have already seen, a proposition must have a sense before the question of whether it is in fact true or false can arise. It follows that the meaning of the proposition as a whole is not something for which the proposition stands, as the meanings of the names which comprise it are things for which they stand. A proposition, in short, is not a complex name. One cannot point to its meaning as something external to the proposition itself. It is precisely this point that the comparison with a picture is supposed to elucidate. The meaning or sense of a proposition is internal to the proposition; it is *in* the proposition as the scene portrayed by a painting is *in* the painting. If the scene portrayed by the painting is imaginary, one may be able to point to objects in the world that correspond to the various parts of the painting but one will not be able to point to anything in the world corresponding to the painting as a whole. Nevertheless there is a scene portrayed by the painting, a possible state of affairs. But this scene consists not in something outside the painting but in the juxtaposition of the elements within the picture itself.

This point may become clearer if we look at two propositions which occur later in the *Tractatus*. At 3.1431, Wittgenstein says that 'the essence of a propositional sign is very clearly seen if we imagine one composed of spatial objects (such as tables, chairs, and books) instead of written signs. Then the spatial arrangement of these things will express the sense of the proposition.' Again, at 3.1432 he says 'Instead of, "the complex sign '*aRb*' says that *a* stands to *b* in the relation *R*", we ought to put, "*That* '*a*' stands to '*b*' in a certain relation says *that aRb*."'

The meaning of the second of these propositions is no doubt obscure, on a first reading. Let us approach it by means of the first. It is evident that we could leave a friend a message not by writing it down but by arranging the books on his desk into a prearranged pattern. The books, so arranged, would form a kind of proposition. Moreover, it will be evident that the sense of this proposition will be expressed by the physical arrangement of the books. That this book stands on the desk in just this physical relationship to that book and the other one says one thing; change the physical relationship and it says something else, or nothing at all. Now similarly the assertion '*aRb*' says whatever it says, because the sign '*a*' stands in a certain relation to sign '*b*'. Change the signs to '*bRa*' and something else is said.

But why does Wittgenstein insist on putting the matter in this way, by saying 'That "*a*" stands to "*b*" in a certain relation says *that aRb*' and *not* by saying '"*aRb*" says that *a* stands to *b* in a certain relation'? His meaning will become clear if we translate the symbols into words. Suppose I say '"The book is on the table" says that the book stands to the table in a certain relation.' A moment's reflection will reveal that I have added nothing to the statement 'The book is on the table'. In short, my statement is empty. Similarly, it is entirely empty to say '"*aRb*" says that etc.' because anyone who grasps the relation in which the symbol *a* stands to the symbol *b* will understand everything I am trying to say simply by being told '*aRb*'. Anyone who grasps the arrangement of the words 'The book is on the table' does not need to be told what it says; he knows that from being told 'The book is on the table'.

In other words, the relation between a proposition and its sense is an *internal* one. The sense of a proposition is to be found in an arrangement of physical signs; it is not to be found in something that *corresponds* to that arrangement, some entity over and above it, whether in the empirical or some quasi-empirical world. Wittgenstein had earlier made the same point in his *Notebooks*: 'In *aRb* it is not the complex that symbolizes but the fact that the symbol *a* stands in a certain relation to the symbol *b*. Thus facts are symbolized by facts, or more correctly: that a certain thing is the case in the symbol says that a certain thing is the case in the world'.[1] To see clearly what Wittgenstein means, suppose that *aRb* (the book is on the table) is true. Then there will be, as we say, something in the world, some set of facts, corresponding to the proposition, which is itself a set of facts, an arrangement of physical signs. But notice that the set of facts which constitute the proposition does not name the set of facts which makes it true. '*aRb*' would have the same meaning even if there were no set of facts corresponding to it; even if it was false. This is what Wittgenstein means when he says that in '*aRb*' it is not the complex that symbolizes – '*aRb*' is not a complex name. But he means something further. For if '*aRb*' is not a complex name, its meaning cannot reside in anything that corresponds to it, whether it be the set of facts which makes it true or some third entity that mediates between it and those facts. In short, if '*aRb*' is true, we have simply two sets of facts, one constituting the proposition, an arrangement of physical signs, and the other

[1] *Notebooks 1914–1916* (Blackwells, Oxford, 1961), p. 105.

which makes the proposition true; and what signifies in the proposition is not some third element but simply its being a particular physical arrangement of the signs 'a' and 'b'. The signs, so arranged, *are* a representation of the world; the representation is not something that lies at the back of them.

But at this point there may arise a difficulty. Let us consider, for a moment, how a picture represents. We may suppose that I have made a drawing of a face. Perhaps no such face exists; I am drawing from the imagination. Nevertheless, we can point to certain lines in the drawing which represent an eye, others which represent a mouth, and so on, the whole representing a possible face. Now there would seem to be no special difficulty in understanding how this occurs, how a possible face is represented by the physical lines of the drawing. Thus certain lines represent an eye because, allowing for scale etc., they look like an eye; and there would seem to be no special difficulty in understanding how the drawing as a whole represents a possible face, for in saying this we are simply saying that there might well be an actual face which, allowing for scale etc., looks like what we see when we look at the drawing. In other words, the drawing represents something because there is, or might well be, a natural relationship, namely that of physical resemblance, between an actual object and the lines of the drawing. But can we say the same of the physical marks that constitute a proposition? It seems evident that we cannot. One cannot, for example, know what the word 'book', or 'table', means simply by looking at it. The relationship seems to be wholly conventional. Moreover, so, it seems, are the relationships between the words in the sentence as a whole. In the sentence 'The book is on the table', the word 'book' is not above the word 'table' but to the left of it. It is true that the arrangement of the words is important. As we have seen, 'The book is on the table' says something different from 'The table is on the book'. But this too seems conventional. If we wished to do so, we could give the first sentence the meaning of the second and vice versa.

But one might wonder whether this proves anything of importance. Might it not be said that we are simply pushing an analogy too far. No doubt a proposition is not just like a picture, but it is like it in certain important respects. Both represent possible states of affairs, the one by being related conventionally to the world, the other by means of certain objective resemblances. But this will not do. For it is evident that Wittgenstein wishes to take the analogy further than this would suggest. For example at 2.151 he says 'Pictorial form is the possibility that things are related to one another in the same way as the elements of the picture.' This remark is meant to throw light on the nature of a proposition and it would suggest that there is some kind of relationship other than a conventional one between a proposition and a possible state of affairs. But what can this relationship be. Obviously there is no resemblance between the words 'the book is on the table' as they lie on the page and an actual situation in which a book is on a table.[2] Moreover it is equally obvious that Wittgenstein cannot be ignorant of this fact.

The answer to this problem lies in what we have described in the first chapter as logical form or logical space. As we have seen, Wittgenstein believed that if an object can occur in a state of affairs, the possibility of that state of affairs must be written into the thing itself. Objects have logical form, or exist in logical space. Now this means that the relationship between a proposition and the world is not wholly conventional. There is of course a conventional element. The marks 'book' might not have been used as we use them, and some other marks might have been used in their place. But the meaning of a name, much less that of a proposition as a whole, cannot be given by this conventional relation alone. Thus one cannot simply as the result of a decision bring about the correlation between a mark and an object, turn the mark into a name. This is implied by

[2] Except, of course, in the sense that *some* resemblance can be found between *any* two things.

Wittgenstein's remark at 3.3, 'Only propositions have sense; only in the nexus of a proposition does a name have meaning.' Correlating a mark with an object occurs only because the mark functions within a proposition. It is its relationship to the other elements within a logical structure that turns a mark into a name, gives it a meaning. Moreover, the logical structure or form of a proposition is not at all conventional. A proposition has logical form when it mirrors the logical form of the world.

But what precisely does this mean? How does the logical form a proposition show itself? The important point to grasp is that the logical form of a proposition is not to be found in the way it looks on the page. The most one can get that way is grammatical form. But, as Wittgenstein emphasizes in the *Tractatus*, grammatical form is often quite misleading as to logical form. In order to grasp the logical form of an expression one has to look at the rules for its use. Expressions which look the same but are governed by different rules are really quite different expressions. To take an example of Wittgenstein's, the meaning of the word 'is' in 'The rose is red' is different from its meaning in 'The Morning star is the Evening star'. The Morning star is identical with the Evening star but the rose is not identical with redness. Again, expressions which look or sound different but are governed by the same rule are really the same expression. We shall meet examples of these later.

But one may wonder whether this gets us any further. For are not the rules that govern expressions themselves conventional? On Wittgenstein's view, only in a trivial sense. It is in a sense a matter of convention that the mark 'is' is used according to any rule at all. What is not a matter of convention, however, is how we can use this mark once we have fixed its meaning by a rule. To see this, let us go back to 'The rose is red'. Given the rules for using 'rose' and 'red', this is a perfectly intelligible statement provided that the use of 'is' is predicative. But now could we retain the normal meanings of 'rose' and 'red' and use not the predicative 'is' but the 'is' of identity? No, we could not. The statement is unintelligible. Have we decided that it should be unintelligible? Not at all. Its unintelligibility follows as a matter of logic from our original decision to use 'is' in a particular way. In short, we cannot choose whatever rules of language we wish, but only those that reflect the logical structure of the world; and for that reason when we have fixed the meaning of a word by means of a rule then how we correctly apply the word in future is determined not by convention but by logic. This indeed is to express the matter imperfectly. It is only if a mark is applied according to rule which reflects logical form that it has been given a meaning in the first place. For it is logical form that confers meaning on a mark and not our decision to give it a meaning. All we can do is decide to use a mark logically. To illustrate this point further, consider the words 'Socrates' and ' – is fat'. These might have been used very differently from the way we do in fact use them. But given the way we do use them, it is not an arbitrary matter that we can say 'Socrates is fat' but not 'Fatness is Socrates'. In the first case we follow logic, but not in the second; and this shows itself, for it is only in the first case that we make sense.

The important point, then, is that the structure which is common between the proposition and the world is revealed only if we grasp the way in which the signs in the proposition are employed, only if we understand the rules for their use. As Wittgenstein says at 3.327 'A sign does not determine a logical form unless it is taken together with its logico-symbolical employment.' This is a point that commentators often neglect because they put the differences between the *Tractatus* and Wittgenstein's later work in the wrong place. Thus they take it as distinctive of Wittgenstein's later work that he denied a name had meaning unless it was used to say something, and that he asked us in general to think of the meaning of a word not as some special entity or psychological process but in terms of its use. Views of this kind, however, are already of central importance in the *Tractatus*. As we have already seen, Wittgenstein denied in the *Tractatus* that a name has meaning except in the context of a proposition. Moreover he asserted at proposition 3.328 'If a sign is *useless*, it is meaningless. That is the point of Occam's maxim.[3] (If everything behaves as if a sign had meaning, then it does have meaning.') Where the important change occurs between the earlier and the later work is in Wittgenstein's conception of logical form. In the *Tractatus*, logical form is something which, as it were, underlies the rules of language and guarantees its intelligible usage. In the *Investigations*,[4] he thinks of logical form as being a kind of formalization of the rules of language and these arise *out of* its use; they do not underlie and guarantee its intelligibility. Common to both works, however, is the view that meaning is not some special entity or psychological process. Thus in the *Tractatus* he is already clear that a proposition at one level is just a set of marks and that what distinguishes such a set from one lacking in significance is not some special entity or process but simply that there are rules for the use of the marks, these rules reflecting logical form, the possibilities of the combination of objects in the world.

It will be useful to develop this point further, by considering propositions 3.1–3.13.

3.1 In a proposition a thought finds an expression that can be perceived by the senses.

3.11 We use the perceptible sign of a proposition (spoken or written, etc.) as a projection of a possible situation.

The method of projection is to think of the sense of the proposition.

[3] This is a maxim attributed to William of Occam (c. 1285–1349). It is usually expressed in the form 'Entities are not to be multiplied beyond necessity.' (*Entia non sunt multiplicanda praeter necessitatem*.)

[4] *Philosophical Investigations*, trans. G. E. M. Anscombe (Blackwell, Oxford 1978).

3.12   I call the sign with which we express a thought a propositional sign. – And a proposition is a propositional sign in its projective relation to the world.

3.13   A proposition includes all that the projection includes, but not what is projected.

Therefore, though what is projected is not itself included, its possibility is.

A proposition, therefore, does not actually contain its sense, but does contain the possibility of expressing it.

('The content of a proposition' means the content of a proposition that has sense.)

A proposition contains the form, but not the content, of its sense.

Wittgenstein is here expressing himself in a very misleading way and a number of commentators have in fact been misled. They have assumed that Wittgenstein is here putting forward a view which he later criticized. Thus, in the *Investigations*, he criticized the tendency to assume that meaning is a special type of psychological process which connects a name with an object and turns otherwise empty marks or words into sense. Some have thought that he was here criticizing an earlier view of his own and that it is precisely in the above passage that the view is to be found. A proposition is merely a set of marks. It is *we* who give sense to those marks by correlating, psychologically, names with objects. But this is not at all what Wittgenstein meant. To see what he meant, we must begin by reminding ourselves that a proposition contains two important features. First it is a collection of elements having logical structure. Thus the proposition 'The book is on the table' has a logical structure which may be symbolized as '*aRb*'. But, second, the abstract structure '*aRb*' only says something when it is filled in with names, when the elements that comprise it are in fact related to objects in the world, when, for example, it becomes 'The book is on the table'. This, in essence, is all that Wittgenstein is saying in prop-

ositions 3.1–3.13. It is only when the elements of a proposition
have in fact been correlated with the world that the proposition
has a sense. Before that it has only the possibility of sense. Thus
'*aRb*' has only the possibility of sense; 'The book is on the table'
actually possesses it.

But, it might be said, it is surely *we* who correlate the
elements of the proposition with the world and, therefore, it is
we who give sense to the proposition. The answer is that
'correlation' is ambiguous. What is obviously true is that a mark
does not correlate itself with the world; somebody has to do
something; some psychological activity is necessary if the correlation is to occur. (What the psychological process might be
is, as we shall see, entirely irrelevant.) Now, if one wishes, one
can call this 'correlation'. But the point is that if by 'correlation'
one means a logical connection then it is not a psychological activity. In short, the psychological activity, though necessary if
correlation is to occur, does not in itself bring about the logical
connection between name and meaning. This is brought about
by the logical structure into which the mark enters. As
Wittgenstein says at 3.3, 'only in the nexus of a proposition does
a name have meaning'. A mark is correlated with an object *only*
if it stands as a logical relation to other marks in a proposition.
This is why the psychological process that might be involved in
correlating a name with an object is entirely irrelevant to
philosophy or logic. At 4.1121, Wittgenstein says 'Psychology
is no more closely related to philosophy than any other science.'
Psychology is irrelevant to philosophy or logic because it is not
a psychological process that gives sense to logical form; on the
contrary, it is only logical form that can give sense to a psychological process, that can make it, for example, a genuine
thought as opposed to a random succession of images. Thus the
psychological activity involved in correlating a mark with an
object is in itself entirely meaningless. What gives it a meaning,
what makes it a genuine correlation, is the logical structure into
which the mark enters. Incidentally, it is entirely irrelevant that

one may correlate a mark with an object without having in mind at the time any of the propositions into which it might enter. Wittgenstein would have said at the time of the *Tractatus* what he said later, namely, that the act of naming makes sense only because there is already a considerable amount of stage-setting in the language. Or, to put this another way, someone can name an object, as it were, in isolation only because he already has a sense of logical structure and knows that there is a place for the name he coins within it. Someone who lacked such a sense would merely be going through an idle ceremony even if the psychological process occurring within him were identical with those occurring within the other man.

These remarks illustrate the importance of not assuming too readily of any view that Wittgenstein criticizes in the first part of the *Investigations* that it is a view he himself formerly held. One should remember that when Wittgenstein re-examined his fundamental views he was at pains to reconsider not simply what he had formerly held but also what he had formerly rejected.[5]

We see, then, in this chapter that a proposition, for Wittgenstein, is a set of physical marks arranged on the page according to rules which reflect logical form, so that the marks, when taken individually, represent objects in the world and, when taken in their full arrangement, provide us with a picture of what might in fact be so. But it might be noticed that Wittgenstein has been concerned exclusively, so far, with empirical propositions; he has had nothing to say about the so-called necessary truths of logic, the propositions that appear, for example, in the symbolic systems developed by Frege and by Russell. On reflection, this should not appear surprising. As we have seen, logic, for Wittgenstein, can show itself only in what is said about the world, about the facts; it cannot itself be stated. This is precisely why Wittgenstein begins with empirical propositions. The only

---

[5] We shall have occasion to return to this point when we consider what Wittgenstein says in the *Tractatus* about solipsism.

thing that may surprise one at this stage is how he can deal with anything else. If logic cannot be stated, how can there be propositions of logic to give an account of? This is the topic with which we must next deal.

CHAPTER 3

THE PROPOSITIONS OF LOGIC

In order to understand Wittgenstein's treatment of the propositions of logic we need to look at a further aspect of the so-called picture theory of the proposition, and, in particular, at the relationship between the sense of a proposition and the possibility of its being true or false.

As we have seen, the sense of a proposition is not something that corresponds to it; rather, for it to have a sense is simply for it to picture what might be so, a possible state of affairs. It follows, as reflection will reveal, that to understand a proposition, to grasp its sense, is to know what possible state of affairs it pictures, or, what it would be like for it to be true, these amounting to the same thing. But, further, to understand what it would be like for a proposition to be true is to understand that if it were not like that it would be false. Understanding what it would be like for the proposition to be false is therefore involved in understanding what it would be like for it to be true.

From this we may see that the possibility of a proposition's being true or false is integral to its sense, not something that occurs as a result of its possessing a sense. The two, in short, amount to the same thing. It will be useful to consider how Wittgenstein illustrates this doctrine in the notebooks he wrote while working on the *Tractatus*. The following passage occurs on page 98 of the *Notebooks*.

Let us consider symbols of the form 'xRy'; to these correspond primarily pairs of objects, of which one has the name 'x' and the other 'y'. The x's and y's stand in various relations to each other, among other relations the relation R holds between some, but not between others. I now determine the sense of 'xRy' by laying down the rule: when the facts behave in regard to 'xRy' so that the meaning of 'x' stands in the relation R to the meaning 'y', then I say that the facts are 'of like sense' with the proposition 'xRy'; otherwise 'of opposite sense'. I correlate the facts to the symbol 'xRy' by thus dividing them into those of like sense and those of opposite sense.

We can illustrate what Wittgenstein means by taking the proposition 'The book is on the table'. Books and tables stand in various relations to one another. A book may be under, next to, far away from, as well as on a table. Now, says, Wittgenstein, one determines the meaning of 'The book is on the table' by laying down that when the meaning of 'the book' stands to the meaning of 'the table' in one of these relations in particular, then the facts are of like sense; in the case of its standing in any one of the other relations, they are of opposite sense. By the meaning of 'the book', Wittgenstein means the actual object for which the word stands. When he refers to the facts of 'like sense' with 'The book is on the table' he is referring to the facts that would make the proposition true; when he refers to what is 'of opposite sense', he is referring to the facts which would make it false. It is very important not to be confused by this. Wittgenstein does *not* mean that a proposition changes its sense when it is false. A proposition has the same sense whether it is true or false. When a proposition is false, it is *the facts* which are of opposite sense not the proposition itself. The reason why Wittgenstein expresses the matter in this confusing way is that when a proposition is false the facts are such that they would be *correctly* described by a proposition of opposite sense. Thus when 'The book is on the table' is false the facts are such that it would be correct to say 'The book is *not* on the table'. But Wittgenstein's point, in essence, is simple enough. His point is that one can determine the meaning of a proposition by indicating what would make it true as opposed to what would make it false. Thus one can determine the meaning of 'The book is on the table' by indicating, out of the various relations in which the book stands to the table, that one set is to be called the book's being on the table and all the rest the book's *not* being on the table. Now the important point, for our purpose, is that the fixing of the sense involves the negative as well as the positive side. There is no correlating of symbols with facts of like sense which is not a discrimination between what is of like and what is of opposite sense. In other words, it is the discriminating what would make it true rather than false that gives a proposition its sense.

Wittgenstein also expressed the point at this time by saying a proposition has two poles, a true pole and a false one. One does not understand a proposition, one does not understand what it would be like for it to be true, unless one understands what it would be like for it to be false. Now properly understood, this view leads to an ingenious account of negation and it will be useful to consider the account here because it will elucidate further Wittgenstein's central doctrine that logical constants do not represent and serve as an introduction to what he has to say about logical inference and the propositions that belong to logic.

Wittgenstein's point is that since to understand a proposition is to grasp both its true and its false poles then negation cannot introduce any new discrimination of fact. If one understands a proposition, one understands what it would be like for it to be false, and if one understands that, then, *so far as the facts are concerned*, one has nothing further to grasp in order to understand the negation of that proposition. We can illustrate this point by considering the puzzle of so-called negative facts. Compare 'The book is on the table' with 'The book is *not* on the table'. The former stands for a positive, the later for a negative fact. But what is a negative fact? One can point to the book's being on the table, but how does one point to the book's not being on the table? Surely whatever one points to will be a positive fact. Thus if the book is not on the table, it must be under the table, or next to the table, or in the next room, etc. But all of these are positive facts: they are not, when taken either individually or even collectively, equivalent in meaning to the book's not being on the table. What kind of fact, then, does the latter refer to?

This is a puzzle that arises wholly from grammar. Compare the propositions when written in the following manner.

The book is on the table.
The book is/not on the table.

The form of the sentences would suggest that 'not-being-on-the-table' is a relation different from but of the same kind as 'being-on-the-table'. To clear up the problem we can write the sentences as follows.

The book is on the table.
Not/the book is on the table.

Written in this way, the second sentence, it should be clear, is not designed to assert the existence of a relation different from that asserted by the first. Its purpose is simply to cancel the first sentence as a whole. One can put the same point in a different way. Suppose we communicated literally with pictures instead of with words. If we wish to say that the book is on the table we hold up a picture of this state of affairs. But how do we communicate that the book is *not* on the table. A moment's reflection will reveal that we do not have to hold up another picture. We can hold up the same picture and then, say, turn it back to front. The purpose of the negation is to cancel a particular representation of the facts not to assert them in its own right.

Now this in a way is Wittgenstein's point. The negative sign (like all logical constants) does not represent the facts. If one understands a proposition one has already discriminated all the facts that are necessary to understand its negation. Naturally this does not mean that a proposition and its negation have the same sense. What it means is that the sense of the negation sign does not lie in the facts; unlike a name, its purpose is not that of being their representative. Wittgenstein made this point by saying that of three propositions p, $\sim p$ and $\sim \sim p$, the third proposition is identical with the first. As one moves from the first proposition to the third one does not acquire more information than one had when one began; one simply returns to where one began. The negation sign merely cancels p; but cancel the cancellation and one is back with p. Similarly if one turns the picture of the book's being on the table one has the negative; turn it again, the positive.

Now what we have considered so far in this chapter is to serve, I have suggested, as an introduction to what Wittgenstein says about formal logic, and especially about the propositions of logic, the so-called necessary truths. At first sight, however, it may be hard to see how this can be so; for, given what has been said, it may now appear even more difficult to understand how Wittgenstein can give an account of the propositions of logic. Thus the propositions of logic are necessarily true, true whatever the circumstances. But on Wittgenstein's account, we have said, it is necessary that a proposition have both a true *and* a false pole; in short, a proposition cannot be true whatever the circumstances. To see how Wittgenstein resolved these difficulties let us turn to his account.

The first notion we must understand is that of a truth function. We have already seen that the names which enter into the propositions of ordinary language need analysis if their logical structure is to be laid bare. As they stand, in their unanalysed form, they are complex structures made up of elementary propositions, the propositions whose names really do stand directly for objects in the world. Now Wittgenstein, as we have already implied, never gives an example of an elementary proposition. What he does, however, is indicate the kind of relation that holds between a complex proposition and the elementary propositions that comprise it. A complex proposition, he says, is a *truth function* of elementary propositions. To see what Wittgenstein means, let us suppose that a proposition is made up of the elementary propositions 'p' and 'q'. Now we have seen that each proposition has both a true and a false pole; in other words, it has the possibility of being either true or false. But in a complex proposition, consisting of 'p' and 'q', the truth or falsity of the proposition as a whole will depend on the truth or falsity of the propositions, 'p' and 'q', which constitute it. Moreover there are various possibilities, various ways in which, depending on the truth or falsity of its constituent propositions, the truth or falsity of the whole proposition may be determined. For example in a complex proposition consisting of 'p' and 'q', both 'p' and 'q' may be true, or 'p' may be false and 'q' true, or vice versa, or both 'p' and 'q' may be false. This can be set out in the form of Wittgenstein's truth table:

$$
\begin{array}{cc}
p & q \\
T & T \\
F & T \\
T & F \\
F & F \\
\end{array}
$$

But, further, the way in which the truth possibilities set out in this table affect the truth or falsity of the proposition as a whole will not be the same for every proposition consisting of 'p' and 'q'. This will depend on how 'p' and 'q' are combined to form the whole proposition. Thus for some combinations, if 'p' is true and 'q' false, the proposition as a whole will be false; for others it will be true. Here are two examples, the third column in each case representing the way in which truth or falsity of the proposition as a whole is affected by the truth possibilities of its constituent propositions:

(A)			(B)		
p	q		p	q	
T	T	T	T	T	T
F	T	T	F	T	F
T	F	T	T	F	F
F	F	F	F	F	F

Truth table (A) is the truth table for the proposition 'p or q' ($p \vee q$); (B) is the truth table for the proposition 'p and q' ($p . q$). Thus 'p or q' will be false if both 'p' and 'q' are false but true for every other possibility; 'p and q' will be true if both 'p' and 'q' are true and false for every other possibility.

This then is what Wittgenstein meant when he said that a complex proposition is a truth function of elementary propositions. The truth or falsity of the complex proposition depends in this way on the truth possibilities of the elementary propositions that comprise it. But let us be sure we have entirely grasped Wittgenstein's meaning. I have tried to bring out in my exposition that a truth table *is* a propositional sign. For example the truth table for the proposition 'p or q' ($p \vee q$) yields as a third column ($T T T F$). Now these for Wittgenstein are *equivalent* signs. In other words, one and the same propositional sign can be written either as '$p \vee q$' or as '($T T T F$)(p,q)'. Or again, either as '$p . q$' or as '($T F F F$)(p,q)'. Or yet again, either as '$p \supset q$' (If p then q) or as '($T T F T$)(p,q)'.

Now replacing a proposition containing a logical constant with a truth table serves to show clearly that the sense of a proposition is equivalent to its truth possibilities. Moreover it serves to emphasize further that the logical constants do not stand for objects, that logic does not represent the facts. As Wittgenstein says at 4.441 'It is clear that a complex of the signs "F and T" has no object (or complex of objects) corresponding to it, just as there is none corresponding to the horizontal and vertical lines or to the brackets. – There are no "logical objects".' It is evident

that the 'F's' and 'T's' in the truth table stand not for objects but
for the truth possibilities of the propositions and it is then
evident that the logical constants, since they are equivalent to
these possibilities, do not stand for objects either.

But granting that we understand what Wittgenstein means
by a truth function how does this enable us to understand the
nature of logical propositions? At 4.46 Wittgenstein says:

> Among the possible groups of truth-conditions, there are two
> extreme cases.
> In one of these cases the proposition is true for all the truth-
> possibilities of the elementary propositions. We say that the
> truth-conditions are *tautological*.
> In the second case the proposition is false for all the truth-
> possibilities: the truth-conditions are *contradictory*.
> In the first case we call the proposition a tautology: in the
> second, a contradiction.

To see what Wittgenstein means, consider the following
truth tables.

p .	$\sim p$		p	$\supset p$	
T	F	F	T	T	T
F	T	F	F	F	T
T	F	F	T	T	T
F	T	F	F	F	T

These truth tables show that we can construct propositions
which are false whatever the truth possibilities of their constituent propositions and others which are true whatever these
possibilities. We can construct contradictions and tautologies.
At 4.461, Wittgenstein says that tautologies and contradictions
lack sense. For example, he says, I know nothing about the
weather when I know that it is either raining or not raining. In

other words, if a proposition is true whatever the circumstances, whatever might occur in the world, then it pictures nothing in particular. But if it pictures nothing in particular then it says nothing, for to say something is precisely to picture, out of many possibilities, some definite possibility in particular. But now it may seem obvious that if these propositions lack sense, they are not really propositions at all. The matter is not as obvious as it seems. At 4.4611 Wittgenstein says 'Tautologies and contradictions are not, however, nonsensical.' This, at first sight, is entirely mystifying. How can tautologies and contradictions lack sense and yet not be nonsensical? What Wittgenstein means is that tautologies and contradictions lack sense in so far as they say nothing, but that nevertheless they are not gibberish. They are, as he puts it, part of the symbolism. Thus in constructing a truth table which yields a tautology one is following the same rules as one would follow in constructing any other type of truth table. There are no comparable rules for constructing gibberish. Moreover, although tautologies and contradictions *say* nothing, they nevertheless *show* something about the nature of logical structure. Thus '$p . \sim p$' says nothing, but it shows something about logic that this cannot be said, or rather, that these signs when put together say nothing. In '$p . \sim p$', one might say, is revealed a disintegration of sense, but the value of '$p . \sim p$' is that the disintegration is revealed by means of it not to be arbitrary. One is aware, by means of it, of rules which reflect logical form and that enable one to construct out of the symbols which constitute it propositions that do say something. Nothing of this is shown in a piece of gibberish, for example 'crunch goo howl'.

Now Wittgenstein's point is precisely that the propositions of logic are tautologies. Here, in other words, we approach from another angle Wittgenstein's central view, namely, that logic can be shown but not stated. The propositions of logic are tautologies: they show logical form but they state nothing about the world. To see this more clearly, let us consider what

Wittgenstein says about logical inference. He expresses his view
of the matter at 5.11:

> If all the truth-grounds that are common to a number of proposi-
> tions are at the same time truth-grounds of a certain proposition,
> then we say that the truth of that proposition follows from the
> truth of the others.

It will be useful to set what Wittgenstein is saying here against
the background of the symbolic systems developed by Frege
and Russell. Frege's system, as we have seen, was laid out rather
like a system in geometry. Certain logical truths were taken as
axioms, or primitive propositions, and from them by means of
certain so-called laws of inference further logical truths were
deduced. When we discussed this earlier we raised the question
of how these elements of the system were to be understood.
How, for example, do the deduced logical truths stand to those
from which they are deduced? Are the axioms in some sense
more fundamental than the logical truths deduced from them? It
might seem natural to answer these questions by saying that
logic, as presented by Frege and Russell, is a hierarchical system.
Some truths are more fundamental than others. The axioms, for
example, are fundamental because they are self-evident, the
other propositions in the system depending on them for their
truth. But there are evident difficulties in this view. For one
thing, the choice of axioms seems to be arbitrary. Thus the
axioms chosen by Frege were of the 'if . . . then' form:
'$p \supset \sim\sim p$' and '$(p \supset q) \supset (\sim q \supset \sim p)$' would be examples,
written in Russell's notation. Russell himself, however, used
axioms which employed the constants 'or' and 'not'. Moreover,
related to this, is a certain difficulty about the so-called laws of
inference. Frege deduced the truths of his system from a set of
axioms by means of the law 'From "A" and "If A then B" infer
"B"'. But what is the status of this law? Does it rest itself on a
self-evident logical truth? If so, is this truth in some way more

basic even than the axioms? Now Wittgenstein presented a view of inference that clears up all these problems. He produced, in Russell's words, an amazing simplification of logical inference.

The essence of his view is that inference rests entirely on the internal relations between propositions. If I deduce that it will rain from being told that there are dark clouds in the sky then there is no internal relation between the propositions involved. The relation here is contingent the inference being justified by past experience. Logical inference is quite different. If 'p' follows from 'q' in *logic*, says Wittgenstein at 5.132, they themselves are the only possible justification for the inference. One can see, in short, that the one follows from the other simply by grasping the sense of the propositions concerned. This is because to say that 'p' follows from 'q' just is to say that the sense of 'p' is contained in the sense of 'q', or, to put exactly the same point in other words, that the truth grounds of the one are contained in the truth grounds of the other. For example here are the truth grounds, the third columns of the truth tables, for '$p . q$' and '$p \vee q$'.

$p . q$	$p \vee q$
T	T
F	T
F	T
F	F

Now the truth of '$p \vee q$' can be inferred from the truth of '$p . q$'. Moreover one does not need to explain why this should be so; one can *see* why it should be so simply by looking at the truth tables. Thus while there are 'T's' in the right hand column where there are 'F's' in the left, there are no 'T's in the left hand column where there are 'F's' on the right. This means that whilst '$p \vee q$' may be true and '$p . q$' false, '$p . q$' cannot be true and '$p \vee q$' false. In other words, one can infer '$p \vee q$' from '$p . q$'.

Now from this it follows that all the propositions of logic are on exactly the same level. If someone deduces that it will rain from being told that there are dark clouds in the sky, he has arrived at further information. He knows more than simply that there are dark clouds in the sky. One may be tempted to view the relation between the logical truths and the axioms in Frege's system in precisely the same way. But this is entirely wrong. In one sense, one never gets further than the axioms, for all that one is doing in developing the system is bringing out what is contained in them. The hierarchical system of logic must therefore be wrong. All the propositions of logic are on the same level and all say the same thing, namely, nothing. In other words, in developing a logical system one is not deducing more and more truths about reality, one is elaborating the internal connections between propositions, showing how their senses are interrelated.

For this reason, also, the laws of inference which are found in Frege and Russell are entirely unnecessary. Their introduction again shows a confusion about the relation between logic and the other sciences. If I know the law that black clouds produce rain then, from knowing that there are black clouds, I can deduce that it will rain. Without the law, I could not have made this deduction; I could not have deduced that it would rain from my observation of the dark clouds themselves. But, as we have seen, if 'p' follows from 'q', one can tell this from 'p' and 'q' alone. One does not need a law. The inference depends entirely on the internal relations between the propositions themselves. This point can be put in another way. Consider the law of inference 'From "A" and "If 'A' then 'B'" infer "B"'. Now suppose I ask 'Why should I do this?' The answer might be that the law rests on the necessary truth '$A \supset B . A \therefore B$'. But do I now need another law to guarantee this, or can I see the truth of the proposition from the proposition itself? If we need another law, we are heading for an infinite regress. If not, then why was a law of inference necessary in the first place? What we have here is merely another expression of Wittgenstein's view that logic differs from the other sciences. Any attempt to prove or explain the validity of logic is inevitably circular; it must itself presuppose the validity and comprehensibility of what it seeks to prove or explain. Logic, as Wittgenstein put it, must look after itself.

It follows, then, that axioms, laws of inference and deduced propositions are all on the same level. Laws of inference are superfluous. Expressed as propositions they are just logical propositions like any other. Moreover what one treats as axioms is a matter of convenience and shows one nothing about logic.

Now, as I have said, the views here being expressed are the views which appear throughout the *Tractatus*, which are fundamental to it. But notice how marvellously they fit into the analysis of propositions as truth functions of elementary propositions. On this analysis, the truth of a proposition depends on the truth of the propositions that comprise it. Logical propositions show themselves in that they are true for all possible situations; i.e. they are tautologies. But this is just another way of saying that logic cannot be stated but can only be shown. Again, on this analysis, logical relations between propositions consist in the ways their truth-grounds are interrelated. This is why there can be no logical relations between elementary propositions, why the truth of one elementary proposition cannot follow from the truth of another. If 'p' and 'q' are elementary propositions, they do not consist of other propositions and, therefore, they cannot have truth grounds in common. But then the truth of one cannot follow from the truth of the other. Logical connections hold only where there is complexity and propositions have interrelated grounds. But this is just another way of saying that logical relations are internal and are therefore to be sharply distinguished from the relations studied by sciences other than logic.

Further, if we reflect on what has been said about the nature of a tautology, we shall see why Wittgenstein thought it important to develop a logical system.[1] Tautologies, we have said, display logical form. Consequently, a logical system, which is a system of tautologies, will display logical form systematically. It will be important to bear this point in mind when we consider the criticisms that Wittgenstein brought against the logical systems developed by Frege and by Russell. At first sight, these criticisms are easy to misunderstand. They frequently take the form of pointing to vagueness, ambiguity etc., in the systems concerned. As such, they may appear to some as being little more than an expression, on Wittgenstein's part, of a passion for neatness, or even of a certain fussiness. But this is entirely to misunderstand their nature. The criticisms follow from what Wittgenstein takes the purpose of a logical system to be. On his view, it is *not* the purpose of a logical system to provide a language more perfect logically than the ordinary. Such a project, on his view, is entirely incoherent. One thing cannot be more logical than another. A thing is either logical or it is not; it is either meaningful or it is meaningless. Thus, the purpose of a logical system is not to provide the logic that ordinary language lacks; rather it is to display the logic of ordinary language more perspicuously than ordinary language does itself. But then it follows that the cardinal sin in a logical system will be lack of perspicuity, vagueness, ambiguity. A vague logical system defeats its own purpose. For its purpose can be achieved only by its being clear.

Now these are points we shall consider in more detail when we turn to a further important feature of Wittgenstein's account.

[1] For reasons that will become clear shortly, it would be more accurate to say that what Wittgenstein wished to see developed was not a logical system, of Russell's or Frege's sort, but a more adequate logical *symbolism*.

CHAPTER 4

THE GENERAL FORM OF
A PROPOSITION

As we have seen, Frege and Russell used different axioms for
their systems, the difference showing especially in their use of
different logical constants as fundamental. Frege used 'if' and
'not', Russell 'or' and 'not'. Now we have seen already that for
Wittgenstein the choice of axioms is a matter of convenience
and shows nothing about logic. He held further, however, that
the mere existence of a plurality of constants was undesirable in
that it obscured logical connections and made them appear arbitrary. To see why he thought this, consider the following inferences:

(a) $(p \vee q) . \sim p \therefore q$
(b) $\sim (\sim p . \sim q) . \sim p \therefore q$

On the face of it, (a) and (b) are distinct inferences; they represent distinct logical operations. But in fact (a) is equivalent to
(b). This is because '$(p \vee q)$' is equivalent to '$\sim (\sim p . \sim q)$'. In
other words, the inferences (a) and (b) would remain the same if
'$\sim (\sim p . \sim q)$' were substituted for '$(p \vee q)$' in (a) and '$(p \vee q)$' for
'$\sim (\sim p . \sim q)$' in (b). What we have is one logical operation
appearing as two; and it is an arbitrary matter whether this
operation be symbolized by means of the logical constant '$\vee$'
and '$\sim$'. But, as we have seen, it is essential on Wittgenstein's
view that a logical symbolism should *not* contain arbitrary
elements. A logical symbolism should constitute a mirror in

which logical form appears with complete clarity, a single
operation in logic being represented by a single operation in the
symbolism. But this ideal cannot be achieved by a logical system
which employs a plurality of logical constants. In any such
system, it will be an arbitrary matter, to some degree, how
logical operations are symbolized.

Now at the time when Wittgenstein wrote the *Tractatus* it
had already been shown that the logical constants could all be
replaced by a single constant — the so-called Sheffer stroke.
Wittgenstein refers to this at proposition 5.1311 'When we infer
q from $p \vee q$ and $\sim p$, the relation between the propositional
forms of "$p \vee q$" and "$\sim p$" is masked, in this case, by our mode
of signifying. But if instead of "$p \vee q$" we write, for example,
"$p|q . | . p|q$" and instead of "$\sim p$", "$p|p$" ($p|q =$ neither p nor q)
then the inner connection becomes obvious.' As Wittgenstein
says, $p|q =$ neither p nor q; and by the use of this device one can
eliminate the plurality of logical constants, thus bringing logical
operations under a single form and representing the inner connections between propositions more perspicuously. For example
'$p \vee q$' and '$\sim(\sim p . \sim q)$' can now be written in the single form
'$p|q . | . p'q$'. This means: neither, neither p nor q, nor, neither p
nor q. It has to be written in this somewhat artificial way to
preserve the neither . . . nor form. But all that is in fact
happening is that one is ruling out the possibility of neither p nor
q, which can be seen on reflection to be equivalent to asserting 'p
or q' or 'It is not the case that not p and not q'.

The point about the Sheffer stroke, then, is that it shows the
plurality of logical constants can be eliminated and therefore
shows also that any symbolism in which they are not eliminated
will obscure logical form. Now this leads us to Wittgenstein's
notion of the general form of a proposition. We can see what
Wittgenstein means by this, if we bear in mind both that
propositions are truth functions of elementary propositions and
that there is only one logical constant. Since propositions, or at
least the propositions of ordinary discourse, are truth functions

of elementary propositions, there must be some way in which they are built up from those propositions. At first sight, one might suppose that the logical constants which appear in Frege and Russell play this role. Two propositions '*p*' and '*q*' become the complex proposition '*p* v *q*' when the constant 'v' is placed between them, they become a different proposition when joined by the constant '.'; and so on. Or to put this more accurately: '*p*' and '*q*' become different complex propositions when subjected to the different logical operations represented by 'v' and by '.'. But this we have seen to be inadequate; for we have seen that 'v' and '.' do not in fact represent fundamentally different operations. Since the logical constants can be defined in terms of one another, can be replaced by a single constant, there must be one fundamental operation which underlies them all. It is this fundamental operation by which all propositions are produced out of elementary propositions that Wittgenstein calls the general form of the proposition.

To understand this properly, however, we need to understand the precise sense in which Wittgenstein speaks of an operation. Let us consider propositions 5.2–5.23.

5.2 The structures of propositions stand in internal relations to one another.

5.21 In order to give prominence to those internal relations we can adopt the following mode of expression: we can represent a proposition as the result of an operation that produces it out of other propositions (which are the bases of the operation).

5.22 An operation is the expression of a relation between the structure of its result and of its bases.

5.23 The operation is what has to be done to the one proposition in order to make the other out of it.

An operation, then, is performed on a base proposition to produce a different proposition as a result. But Wittgenstein has in mind a particular model of how this is done. At 5.2521 he says 'If an operation is applied repeatedly to its own results, I speak of

successive applications of it ('O'O'O'*a*' is the result of three
successive applications of the operation 'O'ζ' to '*a*')'. And at
5.2523 he says 'The concept of successive applications of an
operation is equivalent to the concept "and so on".' In other
words, Wittgenstein is especially interested in operations which
take their own results as a base, in which, as he says at 5.22, there
is a structural relation between base and result. Thus applying O
to *a* one gets O*a*; repeating the operation and applying O to O*a*,
one gets OO*a*; *and so on*. In his later work, Wittgenstein was to
ponder ever the nature of that 'and so on' in a way he never did
at the time of the *Tractatus*. But let us leave this on one side at
present. The point is that an operation can take its own results as
a base. A familiar example is doubling: 2 doubled is 4; take the
result and double again.

Now the fundamental operation (the general form of a proposition) by which all propositions are generated from elementary propositions is of this type. But what is it more specifically?
At proposition 6. Wittgenstein represents the general form of
the proposition as $[\bar{p}, \bar{\zeta}, N(\bar{\zeta})]$; and what this says, he explains,
is that every proposition is the result of successive applications to
elementary propositions (i.e. '*p*') of the operation $N(\bar{\zeta})$. Now
the '*N*' indicates that the operation involves negation in some
way. So what Wittgenstein is saying is that any proposition you
take will be the result of successive applications (i.e. applications
of the 2 doubled, 4 doubled type) to elementary propositions of
some operation involving negation. But what more specifically
is $N(\bar{\zeta})$? This is explained at 5.5.

Every truth-function is a result of successive applications to
elementary propositions of the operation

$$'(----T)\,(\zeta,\ldots)'.$$

This operation negates all the propositions in the right hand
pair of brackets, and I call it the negation of these propositions.

Now what we have in the right hand bracket – 'ζ, ...' – simply represents a particular selection of elementary propositions; what we have in the left hand bracket is a truth table with the F's left out. Thus Wittgenstein's symbol, for our purposes, can be written as $(F\ F\ F\ T)\ (p, q)$. Now what Wittgenstein is doing is explaining '$N(\bar{\zeta})$' by means of that truth table. In short, '$N(\bar{\zeta})$' and '$(F\ F\ F\ T)\ (p, q)$' are equivalent to one another. But that truth table takes us, in its turn, to the Sheffer stroke – neither p nor q or $\sim p . \sim q$. Thus:

$$\sim p \ \cdot \ \sim q$$

T	T	F
F	T	F
T	F	F
F	F	T

So '$(F\ F\ F\ T)\ (\zeta, ...)$' or '$N(\bar{\zeta})$' is equivalent to an operation of joint negation, represented by the Sheffer stroke; and what Wittgenstein is saying is that the successive applications of this operation to the elementary propositions will produce all other propositions. This, in short, is how the complex propositions of ordinary discourse are produced. Consider, for example, how the proposition '$p \vee q$' is produced from p, q, two elementary propositions. If we apply the operation of joint negation to p, q, we get $N(p, q)$ – i.e. neither p nor q. Apply the operation to that, and we get $N(N(p, q))$ – i.e. neither, neither p nor q, nor, neither p nor q, which is equivalent to '$p \vee q$'.

We can see, then, how the essence of language, its common form is mirrored more clearly in a logical symbolism that eliminates the plurality of constants and replaces them with the Sheffer stroke. We shall be returning to the general form of the proposition at a later stage; for the moment, let us consider in more detail what Wittgenstein has to say about logical symbolism:

3.328   If a sign is *useless*, it is meaningless. That is the point of Occam's maxim.

(If everything behaves as if a sign had meaning, then it has meaning).

And

3.33   In logical syntax the meaning of a sign should never play a role. It must be possible to establish logical syntax without mentioning the *meaning* of a sign: *only* the description of expressions may be presupposed.

In other words, a logical symbolism should in itself be a mirror of logical form. It should work not by stating what logic is but by displaying logic in the operation of its signs. For this reason, the hand of the logician should not appear in his system. Having stipulated the rules for how the signs which appear in his system are to be combined, he should withdraw and allow the operation of the signs to speak for him. Moreover this will occur inevitably so long as he has ensured that the rules which govern the operation of his signs reflect logical form. Thus if the signs work, he will not need to state their meaning; this will be evident. For, if everything behaves as if a sign had meaning then it has meaning. If his signs do not work, he will have failed to give them meaning. For if a sign is useless it is meaningless.

It will be useful to illustrate this point by referring to some further criticisms that Wittgenstein brings against Russell's system. One of his criticisms concerns Russell's use of the identity sign.

5.53   Identiity of object I express by identity of sign, and not by using a sign for identity. Difference of objects I express by difference of signs.

5.5303   Roughly speaking, to say of *two* things that they are identical is nonsense, and to say of *one* thing that it is identical with itself is to say nothing at all.

5.534   And now we see that in a correct conceptual notation pseudo-propositions like '$a=a$', '$a=b . b=c \supset a=c$', '$(x).x=x$', '$(\exists x).x=a$', etc. cannot even be written down.

On Wittgenstein's view, the signs in a correct logical symbolism will express their meaning through their use. Thus the identity of an object for which a sign stands should be evident in the identity of the sign and should not need to be separately asserted. Indeed a proposition such as '$a=a$' or '$a=b$', when taken as an assertion about an object, is strictly senseless (to say that an object is identical with itself is to say nothing). Taken as an assertion about these *signs*, it is of course coherent enough; thus '"a" = "b"' can be taken as an assertion that these signs are equivalent in use. But Wittgenstein's point is that in an adequate symbolism this latter type of assertion should be unnecessary. For what is of prime importance in an adequate symbolism is that a sign should signify through its identity, through its having a clear and determinate use. Having to remove an ambiguity, having to explain the use of a sign, in the middle of a logical symbolism is certain evidence that the symbolism is inadequate.

This point is of prime importance in understanding what Wittgenstein says about Russell's theory of types. As we have seen, Russell developed this theory of types in order to avoid the logical paradoxes, which seem to arise if one allows propositions to refer to themselves, or if one allows such notions as classes of classes or properties of properties, or functions of functions. In his theory of types, Russell attempted to restrict the construction of such expressions. At 3.332 Wittgenstein says:

No proposition can make a statement about itself, because a propositional sign cannot be contained in itself (that is the whole of the 'theory of types').

To illustrate this Wittgenstein imagines the attempt to construct a function which constitutes its own argument. Thus in the function 'x is fat' (fx), could the function itself occupy the position of its own argument, 'x'? Supposing it could, it might be symbolized as $F(f)$. But, says Wittgenstein, what occupies these two positions is not *one* symbol but two. Identity of sign, it must be remembered, is not guaranteed by physical shape but by *use*. Marks having very different shapes but the same employment are the same symbol; marks which have the same shape but which are employed differently are different symbols. But in that case when 'F' is outside the brackets it is a different symbol from when it is inside; for it has a different employment. But then we shall not have constructed an expression in which one and the same symbol occurs both as a function and as its own argument. Wittgenstein's point is that in a correct symbolism such a construction will be seen to be impossible and that it is this which disposes of Russell's theory of types. In other words, one cannot in a correct symbolism construct a proposition which refers to itself without making it evident that the contained proposition has a different function from the proposition which contains it. But then it will be evident that one cannot construct a proposition which refers to itself. For, given such a misguided attempt, it will be evident that what one has is not one proposition, referring to itself, but *different* propositions. In short, a *theory* of types is entirely unnecessary. For in a correct symbolism the problem with which Russell wishes to deal simply will not arise. It will disappear in the very operation of the signs.

Wittgenstein has much the same point to make about Russell's axiom of infinity. Russell believed that one had to assume an infinity of objects if one is to guarantee the full intelligibility of one's language; for otherwise how could one be certain there are not, as it were, more names in one's language than there are objects to give them significance? Wittgenstein's answer is that this will show itself in the application of one's language. Where there is an object one can assign it a name; if one's system contains empty names, if there are marks in one's system that lack a corresponding object, the propositions into which these marks enter will say nothing. Either way, Russell's assumption is unnecessary. This answer, as a matter of fact, needs to be supplemented. Russell was concerned primarily with mathematics. His point was that in handling a mathematical system one is *committed* to assuming an infinity of objects, for one knows, on *a priori* ground, that the system can be extended infinitely. One knows, in other words, beforehand that however far one extends the system it *will* have significance and therefore that there must be an infinity of objects if the significance of one system is to be guaranteed. Wittgenstein's answer to this point cannot be fully appreciated until we consider in detail what he has to say about mathematics. Put briefly, however, his point is that Russell has misconstrued the nature of mathematics. For Wittgenstein, mathematics is like logic in that it does not represent the world, and our speaking about infinity in mathematics in no way commits us to making assumptions about the facts. But, as I have said, we shall return to this point later and consider it in detail.

In this chapter, then, we have illustrated the point we were making at the end of the last one. For Wittgenstein, logic cannot be stated, bit it can be displayed in an adequate symbolism. It is necessary, however, that the symbolism be adequate; and we have seen some of the ways in which Wittgenstein thought that Russell's system fell short of this ideal.

CHAPTER 5

THE EQUATIONS OF
MATHEMATICS

We have now considered, in outline at least, most of the central
ideas in the *Tractatus*. But much more detail needs to be
explored. We have to consider now how Wittgenstein deals
with a variety of propositions which, at first sight, do not fit
conveniently into his account. Here are some examples.

1 General statements, containing the words 'all' and 'some'.
2 Mathematical statements.
3 Statements of Probability.
4 Psychological statements; for example, those of the form
   '*A* believes that *p*'.
5 Statements of the laws of nature.
6 Statements of value, in aesthetics, ethics and religion.

The list is not exhaustive. For example, there are also
Wittgenstein's own statements in the *Tractatus*. Wittgenstein
has said repeatedly that logic is shown and not stated, but he
himself in the *Tractatus* is making statements about logic. How
are these statements to be taken?

Let us begin with what Wittgenstein has to say about
mathematical statements. In order to understand this, it will be
useful to consider the notion of a formal concept. At 4.126,
Wittgenstein says:

   We can now talk about formal concepts, in the same sense that
   we speak of formal properties.

(I introduce this expression in order to exhibit the source of the confusion between formal concepts and concepts proper, which pervades the whole of traditional logic.)

When something falls under a formal concept as one of its objects, this cannot be expressed by means of a proposition. Instead it is shown in the very sign for this object. (A name shows that it signifies an object, a sign for a number that it signifies a number, etc.)

Formal concepts cannot, in fact, be represented by means of a function, as concepts proper can.

For their characteristics, formal properties, are not expressed by means of functions.

The expression for a formal property is a feature of certain symbols.

So the sign for the characteristics of a formal concept is a distinctive feature of all symbols whose meanings fall under the concept.

So the expression for a formal concept is a propositional variable in which this distinctive feature alone is constant.

It will be evident to the reader that Wittgenstein is here expressing a point very closely related to the one with which we were dealing at the end of the last chapter. Logic cannot be stated; it shows itself *in* the operation of signs. Thus formal concepts, the concepts in which we seek to express the characteristic of logic, are not genuine concepts, for they seek to express what can only be shown. For example 'It is raining' says something; '"It is raining" is a proposition' says nothing. 'It is raining' shows that it is a proposition, that it is intelligible, *in* saying something. Nothing further is added by trying to state that it is. '*x* is a proposition' is thus an example of what Wittgenstein describes as a formal, as opposed to a real, concept.

It will be interesting to note how this view differed from Frege's. Frege had argued that whether something is a concept shows itself but cannot be stated. That fatness is a concept shows itself in our being able to say 'Socrates is fat' but not 'Fatness is

Socrates'. It shows itself in that the expression for a concept
appears in the predicate position. But Frege did not apply this
view as generally as Wittgenstein. For example, number on
Wittgenstein's view is a formal concept. One cannot say '3 is a
number'. That 3 is a number shows itself in our being able to
combine '3' with some expressions, for example '3 + 5 = 8', but
not with others, '3 is pink'. But Frege himself was quite
prepared to allow a sentence such as '3 is pink'. This goes with
his view that a numeral names an object. It is more evidently
false that 3 is pink than that Socrates is pink but that is not a
matter of logic. Now this takes us to the heart of Wittgenstein's
account of mathematical statement, for in his account he seeks to
show that Frege's view is entirely confused.

Wittgenstein begins his account of number at 6.02 and it is
significant that this comes just after he has given us the general
form of the proposition, the most general form by which one
proposition can be generated out of another by an operation. As
we shall see, he holds that there is an internal connection
between the notion of number and that of the operation by
which one proposition is generated from another. At 6.02 he
says he will give the following definitions:

(1) $x = \Omega^0 x$Def.,
(2) $\Omega\,\Omega^N = \Omega^{N+1}x$Def.

So in accordance with these rules, we write the series.

(3) $x, \Omega x, \Omega\,\Omega x, \Omega\,\Omega\,\Omega x \ldots$,

as

(4) $\Omega^0 x, \Omega^{0+1}x, \Omega^{0+1+1}x, \Omega^{0+1+1+1}x \ldots$,
(5) Therefore instead of $[x, \zeta, \Omega\,\zeta]$
(6) $[\Omega^0 x, \Omega^N x, \Omega^{N+1}x]$

And we can give the following definitions

(7)   0 + 1 = 1
      0 + 1 + 1 = 2
      0 + 1 + 1 + 1 = 3

Laying the matter out in this way brings out the similarity, the inner connection, between number and a formal operation (*a*, O*a*, OO*a*, OOO*a* . . .), one in which the result of an operation is used as a base of that operation. Thus by taking such an operation as represented at (3), or again by taking the form of such an operation (5) we can arrive at a definition of the numbers, 1, 2 and 3. One might express this by saying that the numbers represent various stages in a formal operation or series. Or, as Wittgenstein puts it, a number is an exponent of an operation. By this he means any operation, or, at least, any formal one. Number is inherent in any formal operation; to give a number is to make a stage in such an operation definite.

   Let us try to explain this by means of an example of Miss Anscombe's. We can explain 'ancestor in the male line' by saying 'There's my father, and my father's father, and my father's, father's, father, and so on.' One understands 'ancestor in the male line' when one understands, as one might say, that 'father's' can be added to 'father's' an indefinite *number* of times. My ancestor in the male line is anyone who falls within the series my father, my father's father, my father's father's father, and so on. But suppose one wishes to know *which* male ancestor of mine a given person is. This, as Miss Anscombe suggests, really requires a *numeral* for an answer. What one wishes to know, as it were, is how many times one must go back in 'father's'. Now what this illustrates is that number is inherent in any formal operation. Any formal series is just an indefinite number of applications of an operation to a base. A *number*, 3 for example, is the application of an operation to a base a *definite* number of times. This as it stands, of course, appears circular; for when we speak of 'a number of times' we are already

employing the notion of number and cannot therefore, it might
be said, appeal to it to elucidate the notion of number itself. It is
as if one were to explain the meaning of '3' by saying that it
signifies a formal operation applied 3 times. But the circularity
is in fact entirely apparent, as we may see if we go back to
'ancestor in the male line'. It will be evident, on reflection, that
one can grasp the successive steps 'Father; father's father;
father's father's father . . .' without resorting to the *notion* of
number at all. It is the application of the operation that
elucidates number and not the other way around. This is why
Wittgenstein says that number is the exponent of an operation.
This means that any sentence containing numerals can be
translated into a sentence representing the application of an
operation. For example, '2 + 2 = 4' can be written as
'$\Omega^2 \Omega^2 x = \Omega^4 x$'; and this in turn can be written as '$(\Omega \Omega)$
$(\Omega \Omega) x = \Omega \Omega \Omega \Omega x$'. Here it should be evident that the
appearance of circularity disappears entirely; number is
elucidated by reference to a stage in the application of a formal
operation.

Perhaps the matter can be made clearer still. The point of in-
sisting that number is the exponent of an operation is to
emphasize that numerals do not stand for objects. Suppose I say
that there are two eggs in a jar. This does not mean that the jar
contains three things – one egg, another egg, and two of them.
There is only this egg, that egg, and the jar. Suppose I add a
further egg. I now have three eggs and the state of the jar is
different but the difference is produced wholly by the further
egg. The only objects I have in the jar are this egg, that egg, and
the other one. What then am I saying when I say that the
number of eggs in the jar is three? I am saying that an operation
can be performed with the eggs such that given an empty jar I
can add this egg, O*a*, that egg, OO*a*, and the other, OOO*a*; and
I can go no further. The number of eggs is equivalent to the
operation OOO*a*. For when I perform the operation of adding
an egg to an egg, that is where I get.

Mathematical propositions, then, since they do not represent objects, say nothing about the world. It is important not to become confused at this point. By a mathematical proposition we mean one of the form '2 + 2 = 4', *not* one of the form 'There are three eggs in the jar'. The latter proposition *is* empirical; it distinguishes one state of the jar from another (its containing four eggs, for example). Mathematical propositions may be used *in* discriminating between states of affairs in the world. But the propositions themselves, those which are so used, do not represent any such state of affairs. They represent stages in the application of a formal operation and are *internally* related to one another. In short, they are like tautologies; they are purely formal. At 6.22, Wittgenstein says 'The logic of the world, which is shown in tautologies by the propositions of logic, is shown in equations by mathematics'.

The reason why this point is missed, why it is easy to take mathematical propositions in Frege's way as representing objects, is that logical form is obscured by grammar. The proposition '2 + 2 = 4', in other words, does not display its own form in a perspicuous way and it is therefore easy to take it as an assertion about the facts. But suppose we write it in the form, '$(1 + 1) + (1 + 1) = 1 + 1 + 1 + 1$'. Here the relation between what is on the left and what is on the right hand side of the equals sign becomes apparent. It becomes evident that we are here dealing with an *equation* (a matter of equivalent signs) rather than with a proposition in the normal sense. Or, as Wittgenstein says at 6.2321, it becomes evident that the correctness of this proposition can be determined without comparing it with the facts.

Moreover it is important to grasp the full implications of that latter point. Mathematical equations say *nothing*, i.e., they say nothing either about the world or *about their own form*. Thus we can determine the correctness of '2 + 2 = 4' simply from knowing the meanings of '2 + 2' and '4'. But this is not to say that what '2 + 2 = 4' says is that '2 + 2' means the same as '4'. We

must remember what Wittgenstein has already said about identity, namely, that it shows itself in the operation of signs and
cannot be stated. He makes a similar point at 6.2322. 'It is impossible to *assert* the identity of meaning of two expressions. For
in order to be able to assert anything about their meaning, I
must know their meaning, and I cannot know their meaning
without knowing whether what they mean is the same or
different.' A mathematical equation does not *tell* us that the signs
it contains are equivalent to one another. But then, as will be
evident on reflection, it does not need to do so. For, consider
again, '$(1 + 1) + (1 + 1) = 1 + 1 + 1 + 1$'. We do not need to be
told that the expressions on either side of the equals sign are
equivalent; we can see that for ourselves. In other words,
mathematical equations show and do not state the equivalence
of what they contain.

These points are summed up by proposition 6.234,
'Mathematics is a method of logic.' Notice that this is not to say
that mathematics is derived from a set of logical principles,
which is what Frege and Russell sought to show. Nevertheless
there is an internal connection between mathematics and logic.
On Wittgenstein's view, it is not that mathematics is derived
from any particular set of logical propositions; rather, it is an
aspect of the fundamental logical operation by which any
proposition is derived from another.

CHAPTER 6

GENERALITY

We must now turn to Wittgenstein's treatment of another type of proposition contained in our list; we must consider his treatment of general propositions. It is evident that propositions of this type are of special importance in logic, whether the logic be Aristotelian or modern. Thus, it was Frege's invention of a device for quantifying those propositions — $(x) (fx)$; $(\exists x) (fx)$ — which led to the development of modern symbolic logic.

Now we have seen that, for Wittgenstein, all propositions may be derived from elementary propositions by what is fundamentally one and the same operation. How does such an operation produce propositions that are general in form? One might be tempted to give an account of the following kind. Take the proposition 'All the eggs in the basket are broken' and suppose that there are three eggs in the basket. Then if this egg, and that egg, and the other are broken, it follows that all the eggs in the basket are broken. Generality, one might say, is a logical product. 'All the eggs are broken' = 'This egg, *and* that egg, *and* the other, are broken'. Or, if it is not a logical product, it is a logical sum. Thus 'Some eggs in the basket are broken' = 'Either this egg *or* that egg *or* the other is broken'. One might suppose, then, that general propositions are produced simply by the conjunction or disjunction of particular statements.

A moment's reflection will reveal, however, that this view cannot be right. Take again the proposition 'All the eggs in the basket are broken'. It is evident, on reflection, that this cannot be equivalent to 'This egg, and that egg, and the other, are broken'; for even if these eggs were broken still all the eggs in the basket will not be broken unless there are *no other eggs in the basket*. To state that a particular egg is broken will never get one to the statement that all the eggs are broken, however many particular statements are multiplied, unless one adds the statement that there are no eggs in the basket other than those particular ones.

Moreover we can go further. It is possible to know that everything in the basket is broken without knowing of any particular thing that it is broken. For example, the basket has a label 'Handle with care'. A clumsy porter drops it under the wheels of a train. One may be certain that its contents are smashed without being able to state one of the particular things in it. But surely, it might be said, the general statement cannot be true unless *some* product of particular statements is true. Thus if everything in the basket is smashed then *some* statement of the form 'The tea pot is smashed and the cup is smashed and the plate is smashed . . .' must be true. No doubt. There are connections between a logical product and a general statement. The point is, however, that one cannot deduce from the general statement any particular product. The general and the particular statement constitute different uses of language; they are related but different. Later, Wittgenstein expressed this point in the following way. If I use the picture [o] to say 'the circle is in the square', the position of the circle in the picture plays no part in the meaning of the picture itself. Contrast this with the following use:

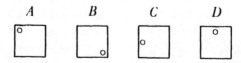

Here I can read from the position of the circle in the picture its position in the actual square. The point is however that [o]

does not belong in the series *ABCD* . . . , *at all*; it is a different
use of a picture. Thus in *ABCD* . . . , it is necessary to consider
the distance of the circle from the edges of the square. In ⟦o⟧
the distance of the circle from the edges of the square has no
meaning, any more than the distances between the letters have a
meaning in '*aRb*'. It might be said that if ⟦o⟧ is correct then
something in the range *ABCD* . . . must be correct also. Certainly; but which is correct is an entirely contingent matter. The
whole point of ⟦o⟧ is that one may use it correctly even though
one does not know which picture in the range *ABCD* . . . is
correct.

I have quoted from views that Wittgenstein held in his later
years. What of his views at the time of the *Tractatus*? I think we
can be certain, from Wittgenstein's own remarks on the subject,
that he was confused on this matter at the time of the *Tractatus*.
What is not at all easy to determine, however, is where precisely his confusion lies.

At first sight, his views seem entirely consistent with those he
adopted later. Thus at 5.521 he says:

> I dissociate the concept *all* from truth functions.
> Frege and Russell introduced generality in association with
> logical product or logical sum. This made it difficult to under-
> stand the propositions '$(\exists x).fx$' and '$(x).fx$'. in which both ideas
> are embedded.

The implication, here, is that generality cannot be explained by
means of logical product and logical sum, Frege and Russell
being criticized for attempting to do so. How then is it to be
explained? Wittgenstein does so by means of the function 'fx'.
Thus at 5.52 he says 'If ζ has as its values all the values of a
function fx for all values of x, then $N(\zeta) = \sim (\exists x).fx$'. As we
have seen, the sign 'ζ' stands for a set of propositions. So,
Wittgenstein is suggesting that by means of the function fx we
are in some way supplied with a set of propositions from which

a general proposition $(\sim(\exists x)\,fx)$ may be derived through an application of joint negation. Moreover the idea is that fx specifies propositions *as* a set, i.e., without going through them one by one. In other words, when we say 'All the eggs in the basket are broken' we specify a set of propositions but we have not arrived at this specification by going through the propositions individually. But how is that possible? What is the significance of the reference to the function fx? Two other remarks by Wittgenstein are relevant here.

> 5.523   The generality sign occurs as an argument.
>
> 5.47   It is clear that whatever we can say *in advance* about the form of all propositions we must be able to say *all at once*.
>
> An elementary proposition really contains all logical operations in itself. For 'fa' says the same thing as
> '$(\exists x).fx.x=a$'.
>
> Wherever there is composition, argument and function are present and where these are present, we already have all the logical constants.

What does Wittgenstein mean when he says that the generality sign occurs as an argument? He is referring of course to the argument of a function, that which occurs in the x place in fx, (x is fat). But if that is what he means by argument, how can he refer to the generality sign as an argument. It would surely be nonsense to write, for example, $f(\exists x)$. To see what he means consider $(x)\,(fx)$. What Wittgenstein is referring to as the generality sign is not the quantifier but the *second* x. His point is that generality is already contained in the x of fx. In the light of this, his remark at 5.47 becomes clear. If we take an instance of fx such as fa (or fb or fc . . .) we shall find it already contains a certain generality. Indeed this involved in saying it is an *instance* of fx; it shares with other instances a common or general form. Wittgenstein brings this out by saying that $fa=(\exists x).fx.x=a$ (a is fat = There is something that is fat and that something is a). That is why it is a mistake to explain generality by means of a logical product (or sum), $fa. fb. fc$ . . . . Since each of these is an instance of fx it already contains a certain generality. But then generality cannot itself be explained by means of them.

It follows then that fx contains generality; it is, one might say, a prototype for a set of propositions – fa, fb, fc etc. But, in that case, it follows also that if we apply the operation $N(\bar{\xi})$ to fx we are at the same time applying it to the propositions for which fx is a prototype; and we do so without enumerating the propositions individually. Russell expresses the matter as follows in his introduction to the *Tractatus*.

Wittgenstein's method of dealing with general propositions . . . differs from previous methods by the fact that the generality comes only in specifying the set of propositions concerned, and when this has been done the building up of truth-functions proceeds exactly as it would in the case of a finite number of enumerated arguments p, q, r. . . .

It will be useful to dwell on this last point. We have already seen how, by applying the operation $N(\bar{\xi})$ to a base of propositions, we can develop truth functions of these propositions. Thus where we have p, q as our base we get $N(p, q)$ – neither p nor q – and by further application $N(N(p,q))$ – either p or q – ; and so on. Now what Wittgenstein has tried to show is that exactly the same process is involved in developing general propositions. Thus if we negate the set of propositions that form the values of fx, we arrive at the proposition that fx is false for all values of x, i.e., $\sim(\exists x)(fx)$. If we negate this, we get 'there is at least one x for which fx is true', i.e., $(\exists x)(fx)$. If we had started from $\sim fx$, we should have arrived, by negation, at 'fx is true for all values of x' i.e., $(x)(fx)$. We see, therefore, that the method for developing truth functions remains precisely the same for general propositions as for the other kinds.

Now this was a point of great importance for Wittgenstein. As he says at 5.47 'It is clear that whatever we can say *in advance* about the form of all propositions we must be able to say *all at once*. Everything in logic is present at the same time; what appears later in a logical system was already contained in what appeared earlier. Holding this view, Wittgenstein is concerned to show, for example, that the notion of negation that appears in propositional logic is not a different kind from that which appears in predicate logic; it must not appear as if there were two logics at work. Moreover this is something that seems to need showing. At first sight, for example, it is not evident that the use of the negation sign is the same in $\sim p$, $\sim (p \vee q)$ and $(\exists x) \sim (fx)$. Wittgenstein brings out the unity by showing that it is the same operation of $N(\bar{\xi})$ which when it is applied to p, q produces a proposition in the propositional calculus $(\sim p . \sim q)$ and when it is applied to fx produces one in the predicate calculus, $\sim (\exists x)(fx)$. Why is it the same operation? Because the only difference lies in the way in which our base propositions are specified. In the first case they are enumerated, specified individually; in the second, they are specified *as* a set. But in both cases, what we have is a set of propositions from which we generate their joint denial by means of the operation N.

It may now seem that Wittgenstein has avoided the error that we mentioned earlier, namely, that of explaining generality in terms of logical product and logical sum. But the matter is by no means as clear as it appears. Russell, for example, after describing Wittgenstein's view in the passage we have quoted, refers on the next page to 'Mr. Wittgenstein's theory of the derivation of general propositions from conjunctions and disjunctions'. In short, it seemed to Russell that Wittgenstein's view of generality was compatible with one that explains generality in terms of logical product and logical sum. Russell perhaps was simply mistaken. But what are we to make of the following passage from Wittgenstein's *Philosophical Grammar*, a work written some years after the *Tractatus*? Under the heading 'Criticisms of my former view of generality', Wittgenstein writes:

My view about general propositions was that $(\exists x) . Qx$ is a
logical sum and that though its terms are not enumerated *here*,
they are capable of being enumerated (from the dictionary and
the grammar of the language).[1]

There can, I think, be little doubt that Wittgenstein is here
referring to the view he held in the *Tractatus*. But if that is so,
how is this passage consistent with the one in the *Tractatus* in
which he criticizes Frege and Russell for introducing generality
in association with logical product and logical sum? How
indeed is it consistent with the general drift of his argument in
the *Tractatus*, where he seems plainly to hold that logical
product and logical sum presuppose generality and cannot
therefore be used to explain it?

To answer these questions, let us reconsider how, in the
Philosophical Grammar, Wittgenstein characterized his earlier
view. He held, he tells us, that $(\exists x) . Qx$ is a logical sum. But
consider what he adds: he did not hold its terms are enumerated
here. It is this latter point which indicates his criticism of Frege
and Russell. In order to arrive at $(\exists x) (fx)$ one does not have to
work through the disjunction 'fa, or fb, or fc . . .' But this is not
because the two are logically distinct. It is rather that $(\exists x) (fx)$
does the work for you. Frege and Russell were wrong not
because they associated generality with logical product and
logical sum but because they *introduced* the notion in that way.
By introducing the notion in association with logical product
and logical sum, they obscured the point of vital importance,
namely, that the disjunction 'fa or fb or fc . . .' presents instances
of a common logical form and is therefore specified by $(\exists x) (fx)$
as a *matter of logic*. To understand generality, in short, one must
begin by seeing how $(\exists x) (fx)$ necessarily picks out a disjunction; one should not begin with a disjunction and attempt to
work back to generality.

[1] *Philosophical Grammar*, trans. A. Kenny (Blackwell, Oxford, 1974), p.
268.

But this is evidently consistent with the view that $(\exists x)\,(fx)$ is a logical sum. Moreover, further reflection will reveal that this view is indeed vital to Wittgenstein's whole position in the *Tractatus*. As we have seen, it was important for Wittgenstein to hold that negation is the same operation whether it appears in the propositional or the predicate calculus. But in order to hold this, he has to hold also that the differences between its use in the propositional and in the predicate calculus consists simply in the manner by which one specifies the propositions to which the operation is applied. Thus one is applying the operation $N(\xi)$ to a base of propositions in precisely the same way whether one applies it to p, q or to fx, and whether one applies it to $N(p, q)$ or to $\sim(\exists x)\,(fx)$. But in that case, apart from the manner of presentation, there cannot be any difference between fx and $(\exists x)\,(fx)$ and a string of propositions, $p, q, r \ldots$, i.e., they must be respectively a logical product and a logical sum. This is why, in the *Philosophical Grammar*, Wittgenstein characterizes his earlier view by saying that the terms of $(\exists x)\,(fx)$, though not immediately enumerated must be capable of being enumerated, and he means 'on purely logical grounds', for he goes on to say that they are capable of being enumerated 'from the dictionary and the grammar of language'.

It is therefore clear that Wittgenstein's earlier view does differ significantly from his later. On his earlier view the truth of $(x)\,(Fx)$ consists in the truth of the logical product $fa.fb.fc \ldots$ On his later view $(x)\,(fx)$ and '$fa.fb.fc \ldots$' are distinct uses of language it being a contingent matter, given the truth of $(x)\,(fx)$, which logical product is to be enumerated.

CHAPTER 7

THE LAWS OF
SCIENCE

It will be useful if we now consider generality under a different
aspect by considering the generality involved in science.

As we have seen, there is, for Wittgenstein, an absolute distinction between the generality of logic and what he terms accidental generality. He returns to this point at proposition 6.3.
'The exploration of logic means the exploration of *everything
that is subject to law.* And outside logic everything is accidental.'
But this might seem to present Wittgenstein with a problem.
For what is he to make of scientific laws, as they appear, say, in
physics? At first sight, these may seem to fit neither into the
category of the logically necessary nor into that of the accidental. In order to understand Wittgenstein's view, we need to
begin by considering the following propositions:

6.31 The so-called law of induction cannot possibly be a law
of logic, since it is obviously a proposition with sense. – Nor,
therefore can it be an *a priori* law.

6.36311 It is an hypothesis that the sun will rise tomorrow:
and this means we do not *know* whether it will rise.

6.37 There is no compulsion making one thing happen
because another has happened. The only necessity that exists is
logical necessity.

By 'the so-called law of induction' Wittgenstein means the
view that what will occur in the future will conform to what

has been experienced in the past. This, he says, is not a law of logic, for it has a sense. By this he means that it pictures a possible state of affairs and therefore, unlike the laws of logic, allows of possible states of affairs that will falsify it. This is why he says it is a hypothesis that the sun will rise tomorrow. Whether or not it is true will depend on what tomorrow brings. In a sense therefore we cannot *know* whether it will be true. This is because the evidence we have for supposing it to be true cannot include what will make it true or false and although there are of course relations between events, none of them is necessary. If one event, for example, occurs before or after another, it might not have done so. This now leads Wittgenstein to his account of the laws of nature.

> 6.371   The whole modern conception of the world is founded on the illusion that the so-called laws of nature are the explanations of natural phenomena.
>
> 6.372   Thus people today stop at the laws of nature, treating them as something inviolable, just as God and Fate were treated in past ages.
>
> And in fact both are right and both wrong: though the view of the ancients is clearer in so far as they have a clear and acknowledged terminus, while the modern system tries to make it look as if *everything* were explained.

Wittgenstein's point is that if we speak of laws of nature, we should be clear we are speaking not of how things must be but of how, as it happens, they are. For example, to say that 'Fire burns' is a law of nature is not in itself to explain anything; we have added nothing to the statement that fire burns. Laws of nature, in short, summarize experience; they do not explain it. By this Wittgenstein does not of course mean that science does not in *any* sense explain natural occurrences. One may explain fire's burning in the sense of linking this fact to others, and, in particular to other regularities. A moment's reflection will reveal, however, that in doing so one leaves the other facts, or

regularities, unexplained. One may of course explain these
further facts, in their turn, by linking them with yet further
facts. But either this process is infinite and therefore can never
be concluded or there is some set of facts which is ultimate and
therefore is itself inexplicable. Either way, it is impossible to
explain everything. For this reason the ancients, when they
explained natural occurrences by referring ultimately to the
will of God, were in one respect clearer than the moderns. For
they were clear that their explanations rested on something they
could not themselves explain and therefore were not deluded
into supposing they could explain everything.

What we have so far, then, in Wittgenstein's account is a
vigorous assertion of the view that physical science is concerned
with the accidental or, better, contingent. Laws of nature
provide a summary of what we have found to be so. One con-
tingency may be linked to another but the process thus linked
remains purely contingent. The matter, however, does not rest
there. For Wittgenstein is concerned to show that there are
some aspects of science that require a different treatment. For
example, at proposition 6.32 he says 'The law of causality is not
a law but the form of a law.' By 'the law of causality' or, as he
sometimes calls it, 'the law of sufficient reason', Wittgenstein
means the statement that everything has a cause. This, he
suggests, is not a law but the *form* of a law. By this he means that
it is not a statement at all, i.e., it does not say anything about the
world. It will help us to understand this if we consider proposition 6.3611:

> ... when people say that neither of two events (which exclude
> one another) can occur, because there is *nothing to cause* the one to
> occur rather than the other, it is really a matter of our being
> unable to describe *one* of the two events unless there is some sort
> of asymmetry to be found. And *if* such an asymmetry *is* to be
> found, we can regard it as the *cause* of the occurrence of the one
> and the non-occurrence of the other.

To see what Wittgenstein means here, suppose I say 'It won't rain tonight because it didn't rain last night and conditions are exactly the same'. Now suppose it does rain. On the face of it, I now have to admit either that conditions are not exactly the same or that something has happened without a cause. Wittgenstein's point, I think, is that the facts can never force us to adopt the latter alternative. In other words, we can never be forced to say that something has happened without a cause because we can always suppose that there is some difference in the conditions under which two events occur. Why is this? Because in so far as we can distinguish one event from another, in so far as we know there are *two*, then there must be some difference between them and this difference we can always treat as the cause of the occurrence of one and the non-occurrence of the other. For this reason 'Everything has a cause' is not really a statement about the world. To say *A* has a cause may seem at first sight to say something definite about *A*. But really it is to say nothing at all. For any difference whatever may be treated as a cause; and *A*, so far as it is a distinct thing at all, is bound to differ from other things.

This point can be made clearer by means of an example that Wittgenstein used many years later. Suppose we take two seeds, one from plant *A* and the other from plant *B*, a plant of a different type. When we examine the seeds we see no difference between them but when we put them into the ground, each turns into a plant of the type from which it came. At first, we should suppose that there is a difference in the seeds; it is just that we have not detected it. But suppose this happened continually and we never found a difference. Eventually we might give up looking for a difference in the seeds. Wittgenstein's point, however, is that this does not mean we need give up speaking of *causes*. For example, we could now treat the origin as the cause. This seed grows in this way *because* it comes from such-and-such a plant; the other grows differently *because* it comes from a plant of a quite different type. Thus the two seeds, just in so far as they are two, must differ from one another in some respect – in position, perhaps, or in origin – and there is nothing in logic to prevent our treating whatever difference exists as the cause of certain events.

Now of course, at the moment, it may seem to us quite arbitrary that the origins of the seeds should be treated as causes rather than some differences in the seeds themselves. But this simply indicates the hold that a particular form of explanation has on us. If A and B have different effects, we expect a difference in A and B. But that is because we usually do find such a difference. There is no proof in logic that things must be this way. Imagine the facts changing and it becomes easy to imagine our adopting a quite different scheme of explanation.

Thus 'Everything has a cause' tells us nothing about the world. What does tell us something, what *is* a matter of the facts, is that we assign causes in the way we do, i.e., in *this* way as opposed to some other. At the time of the Tractatus, Wittgenstein expressed this by saying that 'Everything has a cause' gives us the form of a law; it does not tell us what actually holds. In his later work, he would have expressed this by saying that the proposition expresses something that belongs to our method of representation rather than to the facts that are represented. 'Everything has a cause' gives us a rule for representing the facts. Given the occurrence of a certain event, we are to link it to the occurrence of another. But it does not tell us what links actually hold. At this later time, Wittgenstein held that a scientific theory can be compared in certain important respects with a map. Like a map, the aim of a theory is not to assert something about the facts but rather to present them in a perspicuous way. Like a map also, a theory will contain elements that are *not* empirical. But this is not because these elements are assertions about some world other than the empirical. Rather they are not assertions at all, but belong to the apparatus by which the facts of the world are represented. Thus two maps may use quite different symbols, say, for a town or a railway line and yet present essentially the same facts. The symbols belong to the *way* in which the facts are represented.

This view is already present in most of its essentials in the *Tractatus*, though here he uses a different analogy. Thus at proposition 6.341, he gives us an analogy for Newtonian mechanics by asking us to imagine a fine square mesh across a white paper which is covered with irregular black spots. The distribution of the spots can be described by means of the mesh. We say, for example, 'First square, white; second square, one black spot, etc.' Now it is evident that an equally accurate description could be obtained by means of a quite different mesh – say, a triangular one. They are merely different forms of representation, different systems for describing the world. Newtonian mechanics constitute just one such system. To say the world is such that it can be described by Newtonian mechanics is just as uninformative as to say that the paper can be described by means of a square mesh. For there are any number of other systems by which the world can be described, as the paper can be described not simply by a square mesh but also by a triangular or a hexagonal one.

To some this may appear as a kind of conventionalism, as if Wittgenstein were saying that the facts of the world are determined by the theories we hold about them. It is quite evident on reflection, however, that Wittgenstein is saying nothing of the sort. To see this we have only to reconsider the analogy. It is evident that the facts are independent of our theories and that this will reveal itself in at least two ways. First, although the spots on the paper may be represented in any number of ways, not all ways of representing them will be equally useful. As Wittgenstein says, the spots may be so distributed, for example, that it is much harder to describe them by means of a coarse triangular mesh than by means of a fine square one. Second, even if our choice of mesh were wholly conventional, still the description we give by means of it would not be a matter of convention. Thus suppose we choose a square mesh. Now whether when this mesh is applied to the paper it is correct to say 'First square, white' or 'First square, black spot' is not something that our choice will enable us to determine. Either description may be correct, so far as the choice is concerned. What is in fact correct can be determined solely by the facts. As Wittgenstein puts it:

> 6.3431 The laws of physics, with all their logical apparatus, still speak, however indirectly, about the objects of the world.
> 6.342 . . . the possibility of describing the world by means of Newtonian mechanics tells us nothing about the world: but what does tell us something about it is the precise *way* in which it is possible to describe it by these means. We are also told something about the world by the fact that it can be described more simply with one system of mechanics than with another.

The point then is that science is a mixture of the empirical and the non-empirical. If we are inclined to think of the statement of science as being other than contingent, this is because we are thinking of its non-empirical elements – 'Everything has a cause', for example. The great error, however, is to suppose that this non-empirical element is concerned with the facts. So far as the statements of science say anything about the world, they *are* contingent. So far as they are not contingent, they say nothing about the world but merely reflect methods of representing it.

> 6.35 Although the spots in our picture are geometrical figures, nevertheless geometry can obviously say nothing at all about their actual form and position. The network, however, is *purely* geometrical; all its properties can be given a *priori*.
> Laws like the principle of sufficient reason, etc., are about the net and not about what the net describes.

It will be convenient at this point if we say something about Wittgenstein's treatment of probability. For Wittgenstein an ordinary expression of probability is not a matter of logic. By an 'ordinary expression of probability' I mean a statement such as the following: 'He's usually punctual, so if he said he will be here at 5 o'clock, he will *probably* be here at that time.' Probability of this kind, which gives us an indication of what will occur, is a matter not of logic but of psychology. By this Wittgenstein does not mean that it is *illogical* to make such a statement, i.e., that it conflicts with logic. Rather it is not a matter of logic (or illogic) at all. This is because logic has nothing to do with the facts, with what will or will not occur. Consequently if we are inclined to believe that one thing will occur rather than another, this is a matter of psychology. In other words, it is a matter of what *we* are inclined to believe, as a result, for example, of past experience, of what we have found to work.

So far as probability is a matter of logic, it simply concerns the interrelation of truth grounds. 'In itself,' says Wittgenstein at 5.153, 'a proposition is neither probable nor improbable. Either an event occurs or does not: there is no middle way.' This is to say that probability does not stand for anything in the world. 'There is no special object peculiar to probability propositions' (5.1511). So, if it is not a matter of how our attitudes are guided, it can only be a matter of how the truth grounds of propositions are related to one another. Wittgenstein explains the relation between probability and truth grounds at 5.15.

> If T_r is the number of the truth-grounds of a proposition 'r', and if T_{rs} is the number of the truth-grounds of a proposition 's' that are at the same truth-grounds of 'r' then we call the ratio $T_{rs} : T_r$ the degree of *probability* that the proposition 'r' gives to the proposition 's'.

To see what Wittgenstein means, let us first consider elementary propositions. What degree of probability does one elementary proposition give to another? Since elementary propositions are independent of one another there can be no question of the interrelation of truth grounds. In other words, given two elementary propositions, each alternative is as likely as the other. Consequently, two elementary propositions give one another the probability 1/2

Let us now consider two complex propositions 'p and q' and 'p or q', whose constituents are elementary.

p	q	p and q	p or q
T	T	T	T
F	T	F	T
T	F	F	T
F	F	F	F

Let us begin by seeing what degree of probability 'p and q' gives to 'p or q'. To see this, we have to look at the truth grounds they have in common (T_{rs}) and also the grounds that 'p and q' has alone (T_r). The propositions have only one truth ground in common (T T), and 'p and q' itself only has one truth ground, these coinciding. Thus the ratio of T_{rs} to T_r is 1/1. In other words, 'p and q' gives to 'p or q' the probability 1, which is what we should expect since the former entails the latter.

Let us now look at it the other way around, by considering what degree of probability 'p or q' gives to 'p and q'. We have already seen that the truth grounds these propositions have in common is one. The grounds that 'p or q' has alone are three. The ratio of T_{rs} to T_r is therefore 1/3 and this is the degree of probability that 'p or q' gives to 'p and q'.

We see then, from the chapter as a whole, that Wittgenstein in his treatment of scientific statements holds consistently to his sharp distinction between matters of logic and matters of fact.

CHAPTER 8

BELIEF

We said towards the end of the last chapter that ordinary expressions of probability (as I termed them) are a matter of psychology, of what people are inclined to believe. Moreover this, we emphasized, does not mean that these statements are foolish or incoherent. But this raises an important issue. How do psychological statements, supposing them to be coherent, fit into Wittgenstein's account? At first sight there would seem to be a difficulty. Consider the proposition 'Henry believes that it is raining'. The peculiarity about this proposition is that its truth or falsity seems not to depend in the normal way on the truth or falsity of its constituents. Thus suppose we consider the last part of the sentence: 'it is raining'. This would be true or false without affecting the truth or falsity of the proposition as a whole. For example, it could be false that it is raining and yet true that Henry believes it is raining; and it could be false that Henry believes it is raining and yet true that it is raining. Now this, for someone who accepts the *Tractatus* account, would seem to be very puzzling; for, on the *Tractatus* view, it is essential to a proposition that it be a truth function of elementary propositions. But this means precisely that the truth or falsity of the constituent propositions should determine the truth or falsity of the proposition as a whole. What then has Wittgenstein to say about propositions of this kind.

5.542   It is clear , however, that '*A* believes that *p*', '*A* has the thought of *p*', and '*A* says *p*' are of the form ' "*p*" says *p*': and this does not involve a correlation of a fact with an object, but rather the correlation of facts by means of the correlation of their objects.

It will help in elucidating this proposition if we begin with its last part: '. . ."'p' says p'": this does not involve a correlation of a fact with an object, but rather the correlation of facts by means of the correlation of their objects.' To see what this means we have only to remind ourselves of two propositions we have already considered.

> 3.1431   The essence of a propositional sign is very clearly seen if we imagine one composed of spatial objects (such as tables, chairs, and books) instead of written signs.
> Then the spatial arrangements of the things will express the sense of the proposition.
> 3.1432   Instead of 'The complex sign "aRb" says that a stands to b in the relation R' we ought to put '$That$ "a" stands to "b" in a certain relation says $that\ aRb$'.

As we have seen, what Wittgenstein is emphasizing here is that the relation between a proposition and its sense is not like the relation between a name and the object for which it stands. Thus a proposition has sense because it is an arrangement of signs which, within the arrangement, stand for objects. But the sense of the proposition is not another object. Rather, it is what shows itself when the signs are arranged in one way rather than another. Thus the difference in sense between 'aRb' and 'bRa' cannot be explained in terms of the objects for which they stand; both stand for exactly the same objects. They differ in sense because they picture different configurations of objects and, they do so, because, within each, the signs for these objects are arranged differently. As Wittgenstein puts it in the *Notebooks*, 'facts are symbolized by facts, or more correctly: that a certain thing is the case in the symbol says that a certain thing is the case in the world'.

Now this is precisely the point Wittgenstein is making in the last part of proposition 5.542. The proposition 'p' is a fact, a set of signs. The sense of '*p*' is not an object for which that fact, that set of signs, stands. In short, it does not involve the correlation of a fact with an object. Rather, it says something, and hence can pick out a fact in the world, because it is itself correlated with the world by means of the objects, the signs, that comprise it.

The last part of 5.542, then, is relatively straightforward, given what we have already considered. What is more difficult is the first part of the proposition. In other words the difficulty lies not in what Wittgenstein says about '"*p*" says *p*' but in what he says what the relation of that to '*A* believes that *p*' or '*A* says that *p*'. How can '"*p*" says *p*' be equivalent to '*A* believes that *p*'? Or, to put it differently, how can 'Henry believes it is raining' be equivalent to '"It is raining" says it is raining'? The truth is that they cannot be equivalent. Wittgenstein's explanation is misleadingly elliptical. What Wittgenstein is giving us is not a full explanation of '*A* believes that *p*' but simply a clue to that explanation. The clue is that the relationship between *A*'s thought (or belief) and what it is a thought of is the same as the relationship between '*p*' and what it says.

To see how this can be enlightening it will be useful to look at the account of belief that Russell had put forward a few years before the *Tractatus* was written. Russell had argued that if a man believes that *A* loves *B*, this involves a relation between him and *A* and love and *B*. Wittgenstein objected to this view on the ground that it allowed one to believe nonsense. Consider 'This table penholders the book'. If that cannot be believed it is not because one cannot be acquainted with the elements that comprise it. Indeed it is not even evident on Russell's account why he is allowed to distinguish between one's belief that *A* loves *B* and one's belief that *B* loves *A*; for the elements involved are the same in both cases. On Wittgenstein's view, whatever I am related to in belief, whatever I have in mind when I believe, it must possess structure or sense. This is why he insists that *A*'s belief involves '*p*', i.e. a fact that has logical form or structure.

Now this means that the object of a man's belief, what the belief is *about*, cannot be an object in the ordinary sense at all. The relation between a man's thought (or belief) and what it is a thought of is not an external one, as Russell thought, but an *internal* one, like the relationship between '*p*' and what it says. This is a point especially difficult to grasp in discussing the so-called propositional attitudes. Consider '*A* believes that *aRb*'. There is a strong temptation to hold that what *A* believes is not the state of affairs, for the state of affairs may not hold, nor the mere signs, but some third entity, namely, the *proposition* which is expressed by the signs. The '*proposition*' here seems to figure as a distinct *object* which is related to the man's belief empirically. Wittgenstein's point is that this is a delusion. To believe that *aRb* is merely to have in mind (or to utter) the signs '*aRb*' in their logical arrangement.

To see Wittgenstein's view in more detail let us consider '*A* says that *p*' rather than '*A* believes that *p*'. The problem is the same in both cases but the former is simpler to handle. In order for it to be true that *A* says that *p*, something evidently must be true of *A*. This is the part of the analysis that Wittgenstein omits entirely. Presumably he thought it too obvious to mention. If it is true that *A* says that *p*, it must be true of *A* that he says: '*p*'. More strictly; it must be true of *A* that he says '*p*', or some other set of sounds whose structure has the same logical significance. And '*p*' says that *p*. So we may say that for Wittgenstein, *A* says that *p* = *A* says '*p*' and '*p*' says that *p*.

But now it is of quite vital importance to grasp that the 'says' in the above sentence marks two quite distinct types of relation. In the first, *A* says '*p*', the relation is external or empirical, it indicates the uttering of certain sounds which are in a certain logical arrangement; in the second, '*p*' says that *p*, the relation is *internal*. This is a point that Professor Anscombe, for example, in her introduction to the *Tractatus* seems to miss. She thinks that the relation between '*p*' and what it says, like the relation between *A* and the sounds he utters is straightforwardly empirical; for, she says, '*p*' might not have said that *p*. We might for example have put these sounds to a quite different use, in which case they will have had a different significance. But what does this mean precisely? It is true that the sounds '*p*' might have been used differently. The sounds or words 'it is raining' for example might not have had the use they do in the English language. Given, however, that they have the use they do, is it now a contingent matter that they say that it is raining? The same point applies to '*p*'. Wittgenstein is evidently thinking of these sounds as uttered according to the rules for their use in the language. It is an empirical matter, certainly, that they are so uttered. But when so uttered it is *not* a further empirical matter that they say that *p*.

It should now be possible to state Wittgenstein's view in full. We might express it by saying that when we are told '*A* says that *p*' we are *shown* what *A* says, what he asserts about the world, by being *told* what he utters. Or again, if we are told '*A* believes that *p*' we are shown what *A* believes by being told what pictures occur to him. This is not as complicated as it sounds. The point is simply that *B* can convey to us what *A* says (or thinks) simply by telling us what sounds he utters. How is this possible? Well, first, because these words possess logical form; and second because, since we ourselves have a grasp of logical form, understand a language, we do not have to be told what these say; we can tell that for ourselves.

B's report differs from a normal statement, of course, in that some of the signs contained in it are mentioned rather than used. Nevertheless it is straightforwardly true or false, in that *A* might not have uttered what *B* says he uttered (or have had in mind what *B* says he had). Moreover, where the report does not work by employing truth functional language directly, it works by presenting what shows itself *in* such an employment, so that a report of this type may be explained without in any way going beyond the assumptions of the *Tractatus*.

CHAPTER 9

SOLIPSISM

It will be convenient now if we consider what Wittgenstein has to say about certain further notions in psychology, and especially about the notion of the self. Wittgenstein introduces some of this material into what he says about 'A believes that p'. The effect, it seems to me, has been to confuse some commentators and through them their readers, for they assume that what Wittgenstein says about 'A believes that p' cannot be understood without considering what he says about the self. But this is not correct. The issues touch on one another only at a certain point and, given their complexity, it is confusing to take them together.

At 5.5421, immediately after considering propositions of the form 'A believes that p', Wittgenstein says:

> This shows too that there is no such thing as the soul – the subject, etc. – as it is conceived in the superficial psychology of the present day.
> Indeed a composite soul would no longer be a soul.

To see what this means, let us reconsider 'A believes that p'. This is of the form, says Wittgenstein, of '"p" says that p'. Now, as we have seen, this does *not* mean that on a proper analysis of 'A believes that p', A is not mentioned at all, the real subject being 'p'. What Wittgenstein is objecting to is not the idea of A as the subject but the idea of A's soul as the subject, where A's soul is taken in a certain way, namely, as a non-composite entity. But why does he believe his own analysis shows that the subject of '*A* believes that *p*' cannot be taken in this way? The answer is that Wittgenstein's analysis of '*A* believes that *p*' involves his saying that there occurs to *A* certain psychological elements that possess logical form, and therefore picture or show a possible state of affairs. But these psychological elements in order to possess logical form or structure must possess complexity. Consequently the subject of '*A* believes that *p*' cannot be *A*'s soul, i.e., some non-composite entity. It is easy to see how this leads to a view of the self which is comparable with Hume's. My self is not a simple entity; it is a bundle of psychological elements. These elements are related not to some simple entity which stands, as it were, behind them but to other psychological elements that have occurred earlier or will occur later. I am just this body with that mental history. This view, or something like it, is what Wittgenstein seems to be suggesting, at least on a first reading (as we shall see, it becomes more complicated later).

None of this, of course, implies that *A* is not the true subject of *A* believes that *p*; it merely clarifies what we are to take as *A*, the subject. So far matters seem to be relatively straightforward. They become considerably less so, however, when in a later section Wittgenstein reintroduces the notion of the self in a discussion of solipsism. This section, which runs from proposition 5.6 to proposition 6, is in my view the obscurest in the *Tractatus*, and I am myself very far from understanding it thoroughly. Let us see, however, what we can make of it, beginning with a selection of propositions from the section concerned.

> 5.6   *The limits of my language* means the limits of my world.
> 5.61   Logic pervades the world: the limits of the world are also its limits.
>
> So we cannot say in logic, 'The world has this in it, and this, but not that.'
>
> For that would appear to presuppose that we were excluding

certain possibilities, and this cannot be the case, since it would require that logic should go beyond the limits of the world; for only in that way could it view those limits from the other side as well.

We cannot think what we cannot think; so what we cannot think we cannot *say* either.

5.62   This remark provides the key to the problem, how much truth there is in solipsism.

For what the solipsist *means* is quite correct; only it cannot be *said*, but makes itself manifest.

The world is *my* world: this is manifest in the fact that the limits of *language* (of that language which alone I understand) mean the limits of *my* world.

5.621   The world and life are one.

5.63   I am my world. (The microcosm.)

5.631   There is no such thing as the subject that thinks or entertains ideas. . . .

5.632   The subject does not belong to the world: rather, it is a limit of the world.

5.633   Where *in* the world is a metaphysical subject to be found?

You will say that this is exactly like the case of the eye and the visual field. But really you do *not* see the eye.

And nothing *in the visual field* allows you to infer that it is seen by an eye.

At 5.632, Wittgenstein seems to introduce the notion of a subject that does not belong to the world but is a limit of the world. In order to explain this idea he gives the analogy of the eye and the visual field. The existence of the visual field shows the existence of the eye. But the eye does not itself appear in the visual field. Similarly, the self does not appear in my consciousness of the world simply because it is the *source* of that consciousness and not one of its objects. In other words, Wittgenstein seems here to suggest that philosophy can bring out, though not state, a sense of the self which has not been captured in what has been said about the empirical self; in this sense, the self does not appear in the world of experience, for it is the source of that experience, and therefore can no more be located there than the eye can be located in the visual field.

I say that Wittgenstein seems to suggest this, because it is not clear whether this notion of the self is one that he himself accepts or whether it is one that he considers only to reject. Black in *A Companion to the Tractatus*[1] adopts the latter interpretation. His view is that the notion of a non-empirical or metaphysical self is used by Wittgenstein simply to illustrate the kind of confusion one can get into through not understanding the difference between what can be said and what can only be shown. Wittgenstein himself, however, seems to rely on some such notion in later sections of the *Tractatus*. For example at 6.4311, he says 'Death is not an event in life: we do not live to experience death. . . . Our life has no end in just the way that the visual field has no limits.' These remarks may be taken together with one in the *Notebooks*, p. 77, 'Physiological life is of course not "life". And neither is psychological life. Life is the world.' In other words, in the sense that my physiological and psychological life has an end, my life has no end. By this Wittgenstein does not of course mean that my life goes on for ever. It has no end in the way that my visual field has no limits. Thus while it makes sense for me to ask what is to the right of an object I see, it makes no sense for me to ask what is to the right of my visual field itself. In this sense there is no end to my visual field; it is neighbourless. There is a somewhat similar sense, Wittgenstein seems to suggest, in which my life too has no end. But the 'me', the self, that is being referred to is not an object, something *in* the world at all.

This interpretation, if it were sound, would help us to understand what Wittgenstein says about solipsism. At 5.62, he says that 'what the solipsist *means* is quite correct; only it cannot be *said*, but makes itself manifest.' Wittgenstein is here expressing

[1] M. Black, *A Companion to Wittgenstein's Tractatus* (Cambridge University Press, Cambridge, 1964), p. 308.

himself, it seems to me, in a very misleading way. For example, some commentators have taken him to be saying that although it is a confusion to express solipsism, nevertheless it is really true.[2] But this, it seems to me, is a definite mistake. What Wittgenstein means is that solipsism itself is confused, and not simply that it is a confusion to try to express it. But what then is his point in saying that what solipsism means is quite correct? His point, I think, is that solipsism is the confused attempt to say something *else*, which cannot be said and should be allowed to show itself. There is, as it were, a truth *behind* solipsism, but it cannot be stated and solipsism is the confused result of trying to do so. The truth is not that I alone am real but that I have a point of view on the world which is without neighbours.

We can perhaps see this more clearly if we consider what Wittgenstein says about the limits of language. 'The world is *my* world,' he says at 5.62, 'this is manifest in the fact that the limits of *language* (of that language which alone I understand) mean the limits of my world.' It is important to note the translation of the phrase in brackets. In the original translation, this ran '(of that language which only I understand)'. Translated in this way the phrase gives some support to the view that Wittgenstein was defending a form of solipsism, for it suggests that, on Wittgenstein's view, the limits of language and of the world were given in a language private to himself. But the translation is incorrect; the phrase means, rather, 'the only language that I understand'. By 'the only language that I understand' Wittgenstein does *not* mean German, or English, or Russian. All languages, in the way Wittgenstein is taking them, are one. This is because there cannot be an illogical language. Logic is wholly present in any language that makes sense and a language that does not make sense is not a language at all. All languages, then, can be taken together in that logic is wholly present in each of

[2] This is another example of how commentators have been too ready to assume that a view which Wittgenstein criticizes in the *Investigations* is one he held himself in the *Tractatus*.

them, the differences between them being merely conventional. Now Wittgenstein's point, I think, is as follows. What I conceive of as the world is given to me in language. This conception is the only one there is. I know this not because I have considered other possibilities and rejected them. Rather, I know this precisely because it shows itself in there being no other possibilities. For there is no language but language and therefore no conception of the world other than the one that language gives. This conception is my conception. My conception of the world, therefore, like my visual field, is without neighbours.

But, once again, we must beware of identifying this with solipsism. Thus it is important to remember that my conception of the world shows itself only in what I say about the world. But I have said nothing about the world unless, on the given occasion, it may be other than I have said it is: in short, it is a condition of speech that my language refers to objects independent of myself. If these objects are unreal then so am I, for it is only in my speech about them that my self appears. The self, as Wittgenstein makes clear, is not itself an object. But then solipsism is evidently confused. Properly understood it collapses into realism. For the solipsist in wishing to deny the independent reality of the world, in maintaining that only he and his ideas are real, has the idea of his self as an object standing, as it were, over and against an unreal world. But when he realizes the confusion in this, when he sees that there can be no such object as he takes his self to be, the world reappears as the only reality in which his self can manifest itself.

> 5.64 Here it can be seen that solipsism, when its implications are followed out strictly, coincides with pure realism. The self of solipsism shrinks to a point without extension, and there remains the reality co-ordinated with it.

CHAPTER 10

VALUE

I want now to consider the final pages of the *Tractatus*, which are concerned largely with judgements of value.

As we have seen, a proposition for Wittgenstein is a picture of a possible state of affairs, the proposition being true if what is pictured is a fact, and false if it is not. One understands the proposition if one knows what makes it true and what false. Now, on a first reflection at least, statements of value seem not to be of this form. For example, 'Thou shalt not steal' is evidently not made false if one does steal. One is blamed if one does so, because though one *is* doing so, one *ought* not to be. 'Thou shalt not steal', or 'You ought not to steal', seems evidently not to be a statement of what is the case at all.

This indeed is precisely the view that Wittgenstein held, not simply in the *Tractatus*, but in many of its essentials throughout his life. An expression of value is not a statement about the facts. But, at the time of the *Tractatus*, he held that the sense of a proposition lies precisely in its picturing the facts, or, at least, a possible fact. It follows that there can be no propositions of value.

This is a point that Wittgenstein expresses, towards the end of the *Tractatus*, in a number of different ways. For example at 6.4 he says, 'All propositions are of equal value.' In other words, distinctions of value do not appear in them. Again, at 6.42 he says explicitly that 'it is impossible for there to be propositions of ethics'. The sense of a proposition lies in its picturing what happens either to be so or not to be so. But what happens to be so and what is valuable are distinct. At 6.41 Wittgenstein says:

> . . . In the world everything is as it is, and everything happens as
> it does happen; *in* it no value exists – and if it did exist it would
> have no value.
> If there is any value that does have value, it must be outside the
> whole sphere of what happens and is the case. For all that happens
> and is the case is accidental.

It will be useful to bring out the meaning of this latter
proposition in some detail. Suppose a man doubts the value, say,
of wearing a seat belt in a car. We shall try to get him to see its
value by explaining to him what might happen if he did not
wear one. Here we are explaining what Wittgenstein called
relative value, the type of value that depends on the consequences, on what happens to be so. This is not what Wittgenstein means by value in the *Tractatus*. He means, rather, the type
of value one finds in ethics or aesthetics; and his point is that the
value does not depend on what happens to be so. Thus suppose
someone denied the value, say, of the action of the Good
Samaritan. It would simply be a confusion if we tried to change
his mind by pointing to the consequences of the action. In the
case of the Good Samaritan's action, none of its consequences
could be more valuable than the action is in itself. In his 'Lecture
on Ethics'[1] which was written some years later than the *Tractatus*, Wittgenstein gave a further illustration of this point. If one
tells a man that he ought to be playing tennis better than he is
and he replies 'I don't want to play any better', one would say
'Oh! Then, it's alright'. But if one says to someone 'You ought
to treat your parents better' and he says 'I don't want to treat
them better', one would reply 'Then you *ought* to want to'. The
importance of treating one's parents well does not depend on
something's happening to be so, such as your happening to want

---

[1] *Philosophical Review*, vol. LXXIV (1965), pp. 3–12.

to. In his lecture Wittgenstein spoke of such value as *absolute*, emphasizing again that such values could not be expressed in a proposition.

It is clear, however, that people give expression *in some fashion* to what they value or admire. In the 'Lecture on Ethics', Wittgenstein says that such expressions are attempts to say what cannot really be said. But it is clear, both in the lecture and in the *Tractatus*, that this tendency to express what cannot be said is not, like solipsism for example, the product of a confusion of logic. For example, it is not something to be removed by a proper logical analysis. In his lecture, Wittgenstein says it is a tendency he admires and will defend. Something of importance is shown, even if it is not stated, when a person attempts, in this way, to express what cannot be said.

In this respect, there is an analogy with the propositions of logic; and in the *Notebooks* (p. 77), Wittgenstein makes this comparison explicitly. 'Ethics does not treat of the world. Ethics must be a condition of the world, like logic.' Ethics, like logic, belongs to what shows itself, not to what is stated. This is not to say that it shows itself in anything like the same way. There is nothing in the case of ethics, for example, at all comparable to the method of showing the necessity of a logical principle by means of the *T. F* notation. Still, ethics, like logic, is among those things that 'make themselves manifest' (proposition 6.522).

This can be seen also by considering the relation that holds, on Wittgenstein's view, between ethics and the will.

6.373 The world is independent of my will.

6.374 Even if all that we wish for were to happen, still this would only be a favour granted by fate, so to speak; for there is no *logical* connexion between the will and the world, which would guarantee it, and the supposed physical connexion itself is surely not something that we could will.

6.43 If the good or bad exercise of the will does alter the

world, it can alter only the limits of the world, not the facts – not
what can be expressed by means of language.
    In short the effect must be that it becomes an altogether
different world. It must, so to speak, wax and wane as a whole.
    The world of the happy man is different from that of the
unhappy man.

What Wittgenstein is here suggesting is that the difference
between, say, the good and the bad will is not to be seen in the
facts, in what is brought about, for what the will in fact brings
about is an accidental matter. It is therefore possible, for
example, for a man's will to change, say, from good to bad
without this being revealed in his actions. Wherein, then, does
the change lie? Wittgenstein suggests that it lies not in this or
that fact being different but the world's changing *as a whole*. But
what precisely does this mean? Wittgenstein explains what he
means by an analogy – 'The world of the happy man is different
from that of the unhappy man.' The point is that it is the *worlds*
of the happy and the unhappy that are different not the facts.
The facts, in other words, constitute different worlds depending
on one's attitude to them. So, although the facts are the same,
the good and the bad will confront different worlds. Ethics,
again like logic, is a matter not of the facts but of their
significance.
    We must be careful, however, not to misread Wittgenstein's
analogy. In speaking of the world of the happy man, he is of
course referring obliquely to a common phenomenon. The man
with a happy temperament looks on the bright side, accepts the
very facts that throw the unhappy man into despondency. It is
important to see, however, that this is merely an analogy.
Wittgenstein does not mean that the ethical attitude is itself a
matter of temperament. On the contrary, one's temperament is
just another of the facts *towards which* one has to adopt an ethical
attitude. This is one reason why Wittgenstein, at 6.423, dis-

tinguishes the will which is the bearer of good and evil from the will as a phenomenon, the will that is of interest only to psychology. The ethical will is not a psychological tendency. Rather, it shows itself in what one makes of the psychological tendencies one has, what one makes, for example, of one's happy or unhappy temperament. 'The facts' says Wittgenstein 'all contribute only to settling the problem, not to its solution'. The facts do not solve ethical problems; they can only give rise to them. The solutions are found in the attitudes one adopts towards the facts. But Wittgenstein means *all* the facts, psychological as well as physical. The will, as the bearer of good and evil, is independent of the totality of facts, i.e. independent, in one sense, of the world.

Now Wittgenstein later came to think that there were confusions involved in the way he spoke of the will at the time of the *Tractatus*. Nevertheless, there is much in the Tractatus about the relation between the will and *ethics* that he retained, though in a somewhat different form, throughout his life. In later life, for example, he continued to insist that the facts, though they contribute to the settling of an ethical problem, do not determine its solution. The ethical problem is not to determine what is so but what to do, what attitude one is to adopt. In his later work, he gave greater attention to the kinds of situation in which problems of this kind arise and he was concerned to emphasize, as he never did in the *Tractatus*, the part which the standards of one's culture play in developing one's sense of good and evil. But, for all that, ethical problems remain in a sense personal. Shortly after writing his lecture on ethics, he said in discussion with Waismann 'At the end of my lecture on ethics I spoke in the first person. I think that this is something very essential. Here there is nothing to be stated any more; all I can do is to step forth as an individual and speak in the first person'. And, again, 'All I can say is this: I do not scoff at this tendency in man; I hold it in reverence. And here it is essential that this is not a description of sociology but that I am speaking about myself.'[2] As I have said, Wittgenstein was concerned in his later work to emphasize that a personal attitude develops within the standards of a culture, but he would have emphasized also that such an attitude is not simply the product of these standards. For example, two men who have grown up within the same culture may differ on occasions not simply in what they decide when confronted by an ethical problem but also in what they take to be an ethical problem. What is a problem for one may be no problem for the other. Moreover if one asks 'Which is right?', this question itself requires, for an answer, that one makes a decision on the matter. He expressed the point in discussion some five or six years before his death in the following way.

> Suppose someone says 'One of the ethical systems must be the right one – or nearer the right one.' Well, suppose I say Christian ethics is the right one. Then I am making a judgement of value. It amounts to *adopting* the Christian ethics. It is not like saying one of these physical theories is the right one. The way in which some reality corresponds – or conflicts – with a physical theory has no counterpart here.[3]

In the *Tractatus*, as in the lecture on ethics, Wittgenstein takes questions about ethical value together with questions about the meaning of life, or at least he runs the two together at certain points. Problems about the sense of life, like problems of good and evil, are not scientific problems. 'We feel that even when all *possible* scientific questions have been answered, the problems of life remain completely untouched.' (Proposition 6.52) Moreover, it is not only the facts of physics but also the facts, or alleged facts, of psychical research that are independent of value.

---

[2] F. Waismann, *Ludwig Wittgenstein and the Vienna Circle*, trans. J. Schulte and B. F. McGuinness (Blackwell, Oxford, 1979), pp. 117 and 118.
[3] Rush Rhees, *Discussions of Wittgenstein* (Routledge & Kegan Paul, London, 1970), p. 101.

6.4312   Not only is there no guarantee of the temporal immortality of the human soul, that is to say of its eternal survival after death; but, in any case, this assumption completely fails to accomplish the purpose for which it has always been intended. Or is some riddle solved by my surviving for ever? Is not this eternal life itself as much of a riddle as our present life? The solution of the riddle of life in space and time lies *outside* space and time.

The attempt to make sense of life is not an attempt to determine whether the facts go in one way rather than another.[4] It is in this connection that one needs to consider what Wittgenstein says about the 'mystical'. This word has unfortunate connotations, which perhaps the German equivalent lacks; it suggests a revelation of extraordinary events by extraordinary means. But this is not at all what Wittgenstein had in mind. He introduces the term at 6.44.

It is not *how* things are in the world that is mystical, but *that* it exists.

This is probably related to what Wittgenstein in his lecture on ethics describes as the experience of wonder at the existence of the world. He says there that when he wishes to fix his mind on what he means by absolute value, he calls to mind a particular experience and he says that the best way to describe this experience is to say that 'when I have it I wonder at the existence of the world'. Now Wittgenstein mentions this experience not as something peculiar to himself, or even as something uncommon, but as something with which his audience is likely to be familiar. (The example would have been pointless otherwise.)

[4] This does not mean, incidentally, that facts are *irrelevant* to making sense of things. Imagine, for example, that certain pieces are missing from a puzzle picture. Without them, it may be impossible to make sense of the picture. The point is, however, that the sense does not lie *in* the extra pieces but in the picture as a whole, the extra pieces being necessary because without them the whole cannot be seen properly.

Moreover, it is precisely *not* an experience of something extraordinary in the normal sense. For example, it is quite unlike a case he mentions later, that of seeing a man's head turn into the head of a lion. To wonder at the existence of the world is not to wonder at the world's being one way rather than another. It is to wonder about there being anything at all, the extraordinary here being of no greater significance than the commonplace.

Now it is clear that wonder at the existence of the world might lead one into questions about the sense of the world and of one's life in it. Wittgenstein's point is that these are not scientific questions; but this means, given the views of the *Tractatus*, that in a sense they are not questions at all. This is why at 6.52, after mentioning our feeling that even when all scientific questions have been answered, the problems of life remain completely untouched, he goes on 'Of course there are then no questions left, and this itself is the answer.' 'The solution of the problem of life,' he says at 6.521, 'is seen in the vanishing of the problem.' This does not mean, however, that the worry is unreal, the product of mere confusion, for he continues 'Is not this the reason why those who have found after a long period of doubt that the sense of life becomes clear to them have then been unable to say what constituted that sense?' The sense of life is something that may become clear. But, once more, it only shows itself; it cannot be stated. Anscombe suggests that Wittgenstein might have illustrated this point by referring to Tolstoy, who had tried in a number of books to state what he understood about life. Wittgenstein thought not simply that these represented him at his worst and that he was at his best in a book such as *Hadji Murad* where he sticks to the story but that it was in a book such as *Hadji Murad* that he best expressed what he understood about life. In short, Tolstoy's understanding showed itself in what he said about something else, as logic reveals itself not in what we say about logic but in what we say about the world.

CHAPTER 11

THE PROPOSITIONS OF PHILOSOPHY

There remains one important issue to be discussed. This concerns the nature of the propositions which are found in philosophy and, more particularly, in the *Tractatus* itself. If the nature of logic cannot be stated how can Wittgenstein in the *Tractatus* state what logic is? At 6.54, Wittgenstein says:

> My propositions serve as elucidations in the following way: anyone who understands me eventually recognizes them as non-sensical, when he has used them — as steps — to climb up beyond them. (He must, so to speak, throw away the ladder after he has climbed up it.)
>   He must transcend these propositions, and then he will see the world aright.

This proposition has been interpreted as a tacit admission of incoherence. For if the propositions of the *Tractatus* are nonsensical, how can they be understood, and if they cannot be understood, how can they be elucidatory?

Now it is important to see that the view Wittgenstein is here expressing, though it has its difficulties, is neither as absurd nor as arbitrary as it has been made to appear. To see this, we must note, first, precisely what Wittgenstein says. Note that he speaks not so much of our understanding what he says as of our understanding *him*. He is suggesting, in other words, that even if we cannot, strictly speaking, grasp the sense of what he says, we can certainly grasp what he is getting at in saying it. Secondly, we must take seriously a view which appears at many points in the *Tractatus* and not simply, in an arbitrary fashion, at the end. This is the view that something can be shown even where nothing is stated. Thus Wittgenstein has already said that not everything which lacks sense is gibberish. Tautologies, for example, are not gibberish – they show logical form – but neither do they possess sense. Now the propositions of the *Tractatus* are not tautologies but they belong to roughly the same category. They lack sense, because they say nothing about the world. But they have a point. Unlike the statements of the solipsist, for example, they are not the product of confusion. They have a point precisely in that they may prevent such confusion from arising.

But how, it may be asked, can a statement have a point if it lacks a sense? The person who asks this question, when he thinks of something which lacks sense, is almost certainly thinking of gibberish. But, in the *Tractatus*, as we have said, gibberish is not the only alternative to sense.

It will be important to illustrate this point in some detail. Suppose one shows it is impossible to make a particular construction in geometry. The impossibility involved is of an interesting and instructive kind. For example, it is quite unlike physical impossibility. Thus one may, after a number of attempts, become convinced that it is impossible for one to lift a particular weight. But it was worth making the attempt – that is how one became convinced – and one knows what it would have been like had one succeeded. In geometry the case is different because the proof has the effect of convincing a person that there was nothing answering to what he was trying to do. It is not that the construction is conceivable, though impossible to achieve; rather the point is precisely that it was not conceivable. But then what was the person doing earlier when he tried to construct it? What indeed was the 'it' that he was trying to construct. The difficulty is just as great from the other side. What was the 'it' that the proof of impossibility showed to be impossible?

Perplexity of this kind can arise repeatedly in philosophy. For example, some philosophers (or theologians) have argued that God can see the future directly, and have explained how this is possible by saying that since he exists *outside* time, he can see the past, the present and the future simultaneously; he can see, as it were, directly what for us lies still ahead. It is easy to see what makes this seem plausible. Imagine soldiers marching up the side of a mountain. They cannot see what awaits them on the other side, but someone in a privileged position, in a helicopter, for example, would be able to see both sides of the mountain simultaneously, and would therefore know what awaited on one side of the mountain as they marched up the other. But there is a difficulty, on reflection, in seeing how this analogy is appropriate. The analogy seems appropriate indeed simply because we do not reflect on it. For the difficulty which the analogy is supposed to remove is that of understanding how God can see at once what is occurring at two *different* times. If the times are different, how can they be seen at once, i.e. at the *same* time? It will be evident on reflection that the man in the helicopter does not help us to appreciate this, since it is evident that he can see what is occurring on both sides of the hill only if they are *not* occurring at different times. He can see simultaneously what is occurring at the same time, but if you ask him to tell us what is occurring on one side now and on the other in three years time he will be in no better position to tell you than the soldiers. The analogy conflicts with what it is being used to explain on the very point that needs to be explained. But what then are we to make of the assertion that God can see the future directly. A little reflection will reveal that these words do not (as yet at least) amount to an intelligible assertion at all. We cannot take them as representing even a possible state of affairs. Moreover, that is only half the difficulty. For if the assertion has no sense, how can there be a sense in denying it? What, once again, would be the 'it' that was being denied?

Now there is a point about the sentences contained in these examples that we must note if we are to appreciate what Wittgenstein says about philosophy in the *Tractatus*. The sentences may be nonsenical but they are certainly not gibberish. We can see this if we note a reaction they very naturally occasion. Very many people would be inclined to say, of the latter case for example, that if the assertion and the denial are both nonsensical, still one seems much less nonsensical than the other. For given that it is both nonsensical to assert and to deny that God can see the future directly, it seems a good deal less nonsenical to deny it than to assert it. This is because the denial has at least some function to serve, if only that of stopping the assertion being made. This reaction indicates, though perhaps in a confused way, the point at issue. The point is that the assertion, unlike a piece of gibberish (say, 'Gluck tok hoo'), has an appearance of sense which may confuse people, may take them in, and it may be important to free them from their confusion. This is related to Wittgenstein's point in the *Tractatus*. Thus both the statement 'Logic can be stated' and the statement 'Logic cannot be stated' lack sense in that they say nothing about the world. But the latter has a point, not in relation to the world but in relation to what *other* people are saying; for example it may serve the function of putting an end to a certain type of confused talk, of which the former statement is an instance. Since in its own right the denial says nothing (i.e. represents nothing in the world) it becomes useless once it has served the function, once the confused talk has been brought to an end. So it may be thrown aside like a ladder.

Now, as we shall see in a moment, what Wittgenstein is saying here is not in fact adequate. Given his position in the *Tractatus*, it was not possible for him to make the matter fully clear. But neither was his position absurd. He was dealing with an issue of great importance to philosophy. In philosophy, much error consists not in empirical falsehood but in confusion. Moreover it is important to see that the confusion involved is of a special kind. It is not, for example, a matter of mere woolliness or of a person speaking about something he does not properly understand (though confusion of this kind is also found often enough in philosophy). This is why Wittgenstein says at 6.53 that the correct method in philosophy would involve our demonstrating to a man who wishes to say something metaphysical *'that he had failed to give a meaning to certain signs in his propositions'*. In short, the confusion, with which Wittgenstein is concerned, is a matter of there being something wrong in the use of words. But this is not because the people who use these words are unfamiliar with them, when they are taken individually. In a metaphysical assertion, the words used are often quite familiar ones. Rather, it is a matter of their using words in such a way that they are no longer governed by logical syntax, by the rules which, reflecting logical form, govern the use of their words in ordinary contexts and which ensure in those contexts that they *can* be used to say something. Thus metaphysical confusion is not a result of personal woolliness or of lack of knowledge but of a misunderstanding of the logic of our language. 'The book deals with the problems of philosophy', says Wittgenstein in his Preface, 'and shows, I believe, that the reason why these problems are posed is that the logic of our language is misunderstood.' In metaphysical confusion, we do not notice this because the words we use are familiar ones. It is this which distinguishes them from mere gibberish, which gives them their appearance of sense. One of the purposes of a correct method in philosophy is to remove this appearance of sense by showing that the words in a metaphysical assertion have not been given their familiar use.

It will be useful at this point to return to Wittgenstein's discussion of solipsism, for this is the only detailed example he gives in the *Tractatus* of a metaphysical assertion and of how one should deal with it. The assertion 'Only I exist' (or perhaps 'The world is my world') contains words each of which has a familiar enough use. It is easy to see, however, that the solipsist in his use of these words departs from the familiar ones. For example, on the ordinary use of 'I', the solipsist is just one man amongst others. Thus if I, in ordinary circumstances, wish to refer to myself I do so by distinguishing myself from others, the existence of others being thereby presupposed. The solipsist's point, however, is that there is another use of 'I' in which it refers to an object standing over and against the world in which he distinguishes himself as one embodied person amongst others, this latter world being unreal, being in fact a feature of his own mind. But Wittgenstein's point is that, so far as it makes sense to distinguish a second level in the use of 'I', the word does not stand for an object at all. Solipsism arises because of a confusion between the different levels. It seeks to express a truth, which cannot be stated but can only manifest itself, as if it were about an object in the world. But the self treated as an object in the world is just one object amongst others. In other words, solipsism coincides with pure realism; or rather, it does so when properly thought out. For Wittgenstein's point is that solipsism depends on its *not* being properly thought out. Thus the refutation of solipsism consists not in our showing that the facts are other than it represents them; rather it consists in our showing that no possible facts are represented. Solipsism arises through a misunderstanding of the logic of our language.

It remains true, however, that Wittgenstein's treatment of these issues in the *Tractatus* is not entirely adequate. This, in part, is because he held at the time that there is a sharp distinction between sense and nonsense, that what counts as sense and what as nonsense must be determined for all possible cases. Later he came to believe that the distinction between sense and nonsense, like most distinctions in the language, is not a sharp one.[1] Consider, for example, the difference between night and day. At noon it is obviously not night; at midnight it is not day; but whether it is night or day during, say, a certain portion of the

---

[1] Perhaps it would be better to say that he came to believe there was a confusion in his earlier idea of what constitutes a sharp or clear distinction.

evening is entirely indeterminate. It is much the same with the difference between sense and nonsense. In philosophy this point is missed because we tend to judge all cases by means of those in which the distinction *is* easily drawn. As nonsense, we take a piece of gibberish (Gluck, tok hoo); as sense, a straightforward factual statement (It is raining). What we miss is that any number of sentences may be constructed which fall into neither of these categories. In his later work, Wittgenstein gave many examples of such sentences, the most famous being 'What time is it on the sun?' This question, unlike a piece of gibberish, has all the appearance of sense, and many people when they first encounter it are unable to say at once whether it has sense or not. It is easy to see on reflection, however, that the sentence has no natural application. This is because in order to determine time of day we have to be dealing with a portion of the earth that is illuminated *by* the sun. To speak of the time of day on the sun itself represents no possible state of affairs. Now in so far as it represents no possible state of affairs it is exactly like a piece of gibberish, but in so far as it consists of normal words arranged grammatically it is exactly like 'It is raining', a piece of sense. As we have seen, it is the characteristic of many of the so-called theses of philosophy that they fall into this category: they are neither gibberish nor straightforward sense. They have, as it were, the appearance of sense without its substance. The trouble with Wittgenstein's position in the *Tractatus* is that he could not make this fully clear, because he did hold that there is the sharp distinction between sense and nonsense, that what counts as sense and what as nonsense must be determined for all possible cases. Given a distinction this rigid, it is hard to appreciate the force of what he says about philosophy as an activity which removes confusion, for it is hard to see how there can be, as it were, different degrees of nonsense, how a proposition can lack sense without being gibberish.

But, as I have suggested also, Wittgenstein's view, whatever its difficulties, has certain features which are of real value. In order to summarize his view, it will be useful to consider some of the propositions in the *Tractatus* which are concerned specifically with philosophy.

4.11   The totality of true propositions is the whole of natural science (or the whole corpus of the natural sciences).

4.111   Philosophy is not one of the natural sciences.

(The word 'philosophy' must mean something whose place is above or below the natural sciences, not beside them.)

4.112   Philosophy aims at the logical clarification of thoughts.

Philosophy is not a body of doctrine but an activity.

A philosophical work consists essentially of elucidations.

Philosophy does not result in 'philosophical propositions', but rather in the clarification of propositions.

Without philosophy thoughts are, as it were, cloudy and indistinct: its task is to make them clear and to give them sharp boundaries.

For Wittgenstein, then, philosophy is an activity of a different type from science. But that is not to say it is a pseudo activity, a parade of nonsense. Its aim is to clarify thought, remove confusion, and especially the type of confusion that is contained in misbegotten attempts to speak about the world. At the time of the *Tractatus*, Wittgenstein believed that the major source of such misbegotten talk was a failure to grasp the difference between what can be said and what can only be shown and that once this difference has been grasped confusion could be removed. He believed also that, to remove such confusion, it was important to develop a logical symbolism which was adequate to display logical form.

In his later work, he modified this view in a number of important respects. He became convinced, for example, that formal logic was of only limited value in philosophy and that there was no one source of philosophical confusion, so that such confusion could never be removed once and for all. In other respects, however this view remained very close to that of the

Tractatus. Thus he continued to distinguish philosophy from science, holding that philosophical investigation was primarily conceptual, and he continued to believe that the essential philosophical task was not to establish a body of doctrine but to attain clarity.

CHAPTER 12

THE LATER VIEW

Before concluding this short introduction to the *Tractatus*, it will be useful to consider in more detail some of the differences between Wittgenstein's earlier and 'later work. This will be useful not simply because the differences are interesting in themselves but also because the earlier work may be seen more clearly in the light of them.

We have seen that Wittgenstein, at the time of the *Tractatus*, was clear that the propositions of logic do not represent the facts. It may be noted, however, that they are still in some measure representational. As Wittgenstein says at 6.124, they have no subject matter but they represent 'the scaffolding of the world'. They represent an order of possibilities, i.e. not the world but the *logic* of the world. This point comes out in what he says at 3.342.

> Although there is something arbitrary in our notations, *this* much is not arbitrary – that *when* we have determined one thing arbitrarily, something else is necessarily the case. (This derives from the *essence* of notation.)

The rules of our language are not simply conventional. What is conventional in language, the marks and sounds, derive their sense from the rules for their use, and these reflect the logic of the world. Now the fundamental difference between Wittgenstein's earlier and later work is that in the later work he rejects this idea. In the later work, the propositions of logic

reflect the rules of language and these are found *in* its use; they
do not underlie it. Let us now try to make this view clear.

It will be useful to begin with the general form of the proposition. As we have seen, Wittgenstein thought at the time of the
Tractatus that all possible propositions were determined by the
successive application to elementary propositions of the operation $N(\xi)$. Thus if the operation of joint negation is applied to
'p' and 'q', that determines the proposition $N(p, q)$. If the operation is now applied in the same way to $N(p, q)$, the proposition
$N(N(p, q))$ is determined just as inevitably. Or, to take a
different but related example, if one negates p one gets $\sim p$; if
one negates $\sim p$ one gets a proposition which is equivalent to p.
At the time of the *Tractatus*, Wittgenstein believed that these
steps were unambiguously determined by the meaning that had
been given to the negation sign. In other words, it is a matter of
convention that we should give the mark '$\sim$' the meaning we
do; but what is *not* a matter of convention, given its meaning, is
how it is to be applied. For the meaning of the sign, independently, as it were, of human interference, will unambiguously determine all its future applications.

Now Wittgenstein later came to believe that this way of
speaking expressed an entirely confused idea of logical form.
We can see what he had in mind if we reflect for a moment on
ordinary speech. In ordinary speech the double negation, where
it is used at all, is not equivalent to an affirmative. Thus 'I don't
want nothing' is equivalent not to 'I want something' but to 'I
want nothing' emphatically stated. Moreover this usage,
whether or not it is correct grammatically, is manifestly intelligible. At the time of the *Tractatus*, Wittgenstein would have
said that this is because the meaning of the negation sign has
been changed, i.e. in ordinary speech, the second negation is not
being used in the same way as the first. If it were being used in
the same way then the double negation would, as a matter of
logic, be equivalent to an affirmative. But later he came to see
that this entirely missed the point. For the important point is,

what is to count as using it in the same way? Or, better, what does it *mean* to say that the double negation is determined by the meaning of the single negative? How does the meaning of the negation sign determine its future applications?

A moment's reflection will reveal the force of these questions. We have said that the use of the negation sign is to cancel an affirmative proposition. Now if one adds a second negation ($\sim\sim p$), how is this to be interpreted? Formal logicians find it natural to suppose that if the first negation sign cancels 'p' then the second cancels '$\sim p$', leaving 'p' as the result: the double negative equals an affirmative. But, on reflection, is it any less natural to reason as follows? If the first negation cancels 'p', the second repeats the cancellation of 'p' with double force. Why, in short, should we suppose that the second negation sign cancels '$\sim p$'? Why should we not follow ordinary speech in taking the second negation sign as applying with the first to 'p'? The unbiased mind will discover on reflection that those who follow ordinary speech have as much reason as their opponents to claim that they are using the second negation sign in the same way as the first. But in that case how can the meaning of the negation sign determine unambiguously its future applications?

Now this point, once grasped, will lead one to reflect on what is meant by saying that the meaning of a sign determines its future applications. This is a phrase that comes naturally to one in certain circumstances. For example, when one considers the steps of a mathematical series (say, 2, 4, 6, 8 . . .), one may have the feeling that the further steps are already determined; even if we have not yet drawn them, they are, as it were, waiting to be drawn. It is as if when we write down the steps we are merely tracing over what in some sense already exists. This is not quite the idea that Wittgenstein had at the time of the *Tractatus*. As we have seen, he was clear that the steps of the series do not exist as objects. Nevertheless, the *possibility* of the steps, he felt, is in some sense determined by the earlier steps, quite independently of what any person who is continuing the series happens to write down. But the question is, in what sense determined? It is this idea of being determined logically which is left obscure in the *Tractatus*, and to which he devotes himself in his later work.

In order to clarify this, let us consider an example that Wittgenstein himself used later. From '$(X) fx$' (everything is f) it follows that fa (that some particular thing, a, is f). If everything on the table is red, for example, it follows that this apple, which is on the table, is red. But why does this follow? Or, rather, in *what sense* does it do so? One may be inclined to say that it follows from the *meaning* of '$(X) fx$'. Anyone who understands the meaning of '$(X) fx$' is *bound* to admit that 'fa' follows. But in what sense 'bound'? Wittgenstein in his later work said that this would be clarified if it were expressed by saying not that the meaning of '$(X) fx$' determines that 'fa' follows but that anyone who did not see that he should infer 'fa' from '$(X) fx$' would not be said to have grasped the meaning of '$(X) fx$'. In other words, we should be prepared to say of someone that he understands 'Everything on the table is red' only if, in asserting it, he were prepared to asert of any given thing on the table (this apple, for example) that it is red. Asserting the latter is a condition for asserting the former. Or, to put that another way, '$(X) fx$ entails fa' may be treated as a *rule* for the use of '$(X) fx$'. Thus the statement that the meaning of '$(X) fx$' determines that fa follows is true only in the sense that our inferring 'fa' from '$(X) fx$' determines the meaning of $(X) fx$. The same point applies in the case of the logical constants. Thus from '$p \lor q$ and $\sim q$' it follows that p. In what sense does it follow? Well, is it not clear that someone asserting 'p or q' must *already* be prepared, if we are to understand him, to assert that if one of these propositions is false, 'q' for example, the other is true? In other words, the latter follows from the former only in the sense that it is a condition for asserting it.

Now Wittgenstein does in fact come close to saying this in the *Tractatus*. But in the *Tractatus* a proposition, such as 'p or q',

is generated by means of an operation on elementary propositions. It derives its sense from its position within the system
of propositions, of intelligible statements. In the later work, this
idea is cast aside. Language does not form a system, in the sense
of a calculus. If we wish to know how we get a proposition such
as 'p or q', we should look in a quite different place; we should
look at the purpose it serves, the place it has, within the activities
of a social life. As I have said, '$(X)fx \supset fa$' and '$p \vee q \cdot \sim q \therefore p$'
may be regarded as rules for the use of '$(X)fx$ and '$p \vee q$' respectively. But these rules are not the reflection of some deeper lying
logical structure. The propositions of logic do not reflect what
underlies the rules but are a crystallization of the rules
themselves, these rules deriving their point from what sur-
rounds them, the social life into which they enter.

But let us pause; for, to some, the above analysis will seem to
contain an obvious flaw. We have said that the inferences which
follow, for example, from the logical constants are really an
expression of the meaning of these constants. But this may seem
plausible only if we confine ourselves to simple cases. It becomes
less plausible, so the argument would run, if we consider the inferences that run through a logical system as a whole. For it is
evident that many of these inferences have yet to be drawn. But
in that case, how can these inferences, as yet undrawn, be part of
the meaning of the logical constants? Surely, we must first
determine the meaning of the constants before we can go on and
draw further inferences. But then what account are we to give
of how these further inferences follow from the meaning of the
logical constants? One answer to this problem has been much
criticized. It has been said by certain of the logical positivists
(philosophers who, as it happens, were influenced in certain
respects by the *Tractatus*) that a logical system may be divided, as
it were, into two parts. The meaning of the signs used in the
early part of our system is determined by the rules we give
them, the rest of the system consists of what follows from our
rules. But this, it has been said, is no solution whatever. For how

are we to understand the phrase 'follows from our rules'? It seems there are only two possibilities. Either the logical positivists are forced to appeal to a notion they should be elucidating, namely, that of a logical structure which, existing independently of empirical facts and human agreement, guarantees the development of our system, or, they are forced to suppose that the development of a logical system is entirely arbitrary, depending at any given point on how we happen to feel like developing it. But the first alternative begs the question and the second seems wildly implausible.

Now it is important to see that this problem is entirely apparent. Properly understood, it disappears. To see this, it will be useful to consider an analogy. Computers can be constructed which will agree in providing the answers to problems that, at the time, no human being has as much as considered. How is this possible? It seems evident that the computers have no grasp of logical principles, that they work, in short, according to purely natural causes. To this it might be said that the engineers who build the computers do have a grasp of such principles and they build computers to work in conformity with them. But on reflection it will be seen that this is no answer to the problem. For how do the engineers build into the computers the way to apply these principles to problems that the engineers themselves have never even considered? How is it that two computers working independently of one another can agree in the solution to a problem, the solution, as yet, not having been seen by human eye?

Now is it not evident, on reflection, that what we have here is merely the illusion of a problem? The computers agree because they were built along the same lines. The rest is merely the workings of natural causation. An explanation analogous to this applies in the case of human beings developing a logical or mathematical system. People who have been taught to use signs in certain ways will continue, in different circumstances, to agree in their use of these signs, even when they are working in-

dependently of one another. The explanation for this (if
explanation be needed) lies in the way they were trained in the
first place. It is just a fact that people who have received the
same training in certain circumstances will react similarly in
others, not as a result of explicit agreement but as a result of their
training. The development of a logical or mathematical system
depends on this agreement in reaction. In other words, the
development of a logical or mathematical system is neither, in
any natural sense of the word, an arbitrary matter, nor is it a
matter of being guided by some underlying logical structure.
Logical principles, in fact, are not themselves factors in
explaining the development of a system; which is not to deny
that logical principles exist but rather to elucidate their nature.
Logical principles are a feature of the system once developed,
not factors required in the explanation of how the development
occurs.

This point will be further clarified if we compare the
development of a system in logic or in mathematics with composing variations on a theme in music, this being one of
Wittgenstein's favourite analogies. The theme will represent
the first part of the system, the variations its development. The
analogy is a good one for Wittgenstein's purpose because it
would be entirely implausible to maintain either that a theme
determines its own variations (independently, as it were, of
human interference, of how it strikes the composer) or that the
variation form in music is entirely arbitrary, the composer being
free to write down just whatever happens to come into his head.
Thus it seems evident that the man who composes variations on
a theme is as much a creator as a discoverer, and that one set of
variations does not exclude another set, which is equally good,
on the same theme. There is a theme of Paganini's, for example,
which is the subject of countless variations by different com-
posers, Brahms alone writing two such sets. Obviously it would
be foolish to maintain that there is only one correct set of such
variations. But then it would be equally foolish to maintain that

it is entirely arbitrary how a variation is composed. If we see no connection between a theme and its variation, we do not say the composer has written a bad variation; we say he has written no variation at all. Most of us, for example, when we first hear the most famous of Rachmaninov's variations on Paganini's theme, can detect no connection with the theme itself. The connection is that the variation presents the theme in inversion. When we are convinced of this we allow that Rachmaninov has written a variation as opposed simply to having written a good tune. In other words, a theme counts as a variation on another only if there is some connection between them.

But this raises an important point. Is it not possible to find *some* connection between any two things? For example, suppose that Rachmaninov had inserted 'God Save the Queen' as one of the variations on the Paganini theme and, when questioned about this, had said that he first heard Paganini's theme during a concert at which the Queen of England was present. We shoud. not accept, on this ground, that he had written a variation. Nevertheless there would be a connection, of sorts, between what he wrote and Paganini's theme. Similarly, suppose I continue the series, 2, 4, 6, 8 . . . by writing down 14; this is because my eldest child is fourteen, my other children being aged respectively two, four, six and eight. This would not count as continuing the series. On the other hand, it counts as continuing the series if I write down 10, my reason being that this is the fifth even number of the cardinal number series, the preceding four even numbers constituting the beginning of the series I seek to continue. But why should this be? In both cases there is a connection. It seems that in order to compose a variation or continue a mathematical series I must find not simply a connection with what precedes it, but a connection that is pertinent. This, however, may seem to surrender the whole position. For how is it possible to explain what makes a connection pertinent without appealing to something other than the ordinary facts and the reactions of the practitioners. As a matter of fact, it is easy to do so. It is easy to show that what makes a connection pertinent is not something which underlies a practice; rather it is settled by the reactions of the practitioners themselves. Thus if the connection between Paganini's theme and the Queen of England is entirely personal to the man who is writing the variations then it will not count as a variation if he inserts 'God Save the Queen'. But suppose it were a well known fact, something familiar to all music lovers, that Paganini's theme was written at the request of a British monarch who appeared at its first performance; it would then be entirely acceptable for a composer to include at least a passing reference to the British national anthem in his variations on that theme. Similarly, in continuing a mathematical series I am not supposed to consider the ages of my children. Rather, I am supposed to consider only those factors which are common to those who have been trained in mathematics. A training in mathematics is itself of course precisely an attempt to concentrate the pupil's attention on some factors to the exclusion of others. This is why what is suggested to someone who has undergone such a training and who is asked to concentrate on something falling within the range will almost certainly be identical with what is suggested to someone else who concentrates on these factors and has undergone the same training. In this way mathematicians reach agreement and a mathematical system is developed. In short, what makes something a correct step in composing a variation or in continuing a series is that it is connected pertinently with what precedes it; what makes a connection pertinent is settled by the reactions of the practitioners.

Perhaps the matter can be made simpler still. Consider the relation between Paganini's theme and the most famous of Rachmaninov's variations. In the variations, as we have said, the theme appears in inversion. The precise meaning of this is unimportant. It is sufficient that it refers to some fact about the two tunes which is as objective as any other. But what makes such a fact relevant in composing a variation? Simply, that there is an

activity in which people are led, whether or not by explicit
training, to treat such facts as relevant and it is this activity that
we call composing variations. Similarly, the series, 2, 4, 6, 8
. . ., is constituted by what is in fact the first four even numbers
in the series of cardinal numbers (or, every other number in that
series). The numbers, 10, 12, 14 . . ., continue the series of even
numbers. But what makes these facts relevent in continuing a
mathematical series? Simply, that there is an activity in which
people are trained to treat such facts as relevant and it is this
activity we call mathematics, It is not mathematics that determines what is relevant, i.e., something which underlies the
human practice. Rather, it is the fact that those who take part in
a particular practice (or set of practices) treat one thing as
relevant rather than another which defines mathematics. Thus
the facts to which mathematics refer would not in themselves
produce mathematics. In addition there must be mathematicians
to react to these facts. Out of the interaction between the two
mathematics arises. In short, one may say that what makes
mathematics non-arbitrary is that mathematicians are not arbitrary in their responses; they respond in ways that confirm
what they expect of one another; and the explanation for this is
to be found, if it is to be found at all, in certain general facts
about human and physical nature.

The reason why these points are overlooked is that our sense
of what is relevant or appropriate, not simply in mathematics
and music but in social life generally, is often influenced by
factors we have forgotten or of which were hardly even aware,
and, then, when we philosophize we are inclined to suppose
that the factors that influenced it exist independently of human
activity altogether.[1] Wittgenstein gives an excellent illustration

---

[1] This is related to what Marx had in mind when he spoke of alienation.
The word 'alienation' has by now become meaningless, but Marx used it to
express an important insight. Thus he noted a tendency to attribute, as it
were, to the nature of things what is really the product of people's own
actions. For example, people sometimes believe, or act as if they believed,

in the *Investigations* of how tacitly we rely on what is relevant or appropriate. Suppose we ask someone to teach our children a game. When we return, we find he is teaching them a gambling game, say, roulette or blackjack. Indignantly we say 'That is not what we meant by a game'. Why are we justified in our indignation. After all, roulette and blackjack are classified as games. Moreover we did not exclude them in what we said, and it is entirely unlikely that we even excluded them mentally when we said it. The reason is that in this context such things go without saying. Not only is it inappropriate to teach children such a game, it is normally inappropriate to tell someone not to do so. Acquiring this sense of what it is appropriate to say or do is the most important part of learning a language, a knowledge of grammatical structure being, by comparison, of minor im-

---

that the workings of the state or of the economic system are something more than the activities of those who comprise the state or carry on economic affairs; indeed it is almost as though they believed that the activities of those who comprise the state or carry on economic affairs could be explained by the workings of, as it were, the State or of the Economic System. They treat the products of their own activity as if they were alien to them. A follower of Marx once satirized this tendency by saying that in addition to considering the interests of patients and doctors we must be careful not to neglect the interests of Medicine. This view was vulgarized by later Marxists who, unlike Marx, failed to keep in mind two equally important points, namely (a) that medicine, for example, does not exist independently of the actions of patients and doctors and (b) that the relation between a patient and a doctor is not something that can be altered at will. It is (b) in fact that helps to explain the tendency to treat Medicine as if it existed independently of patients and doctors. The point is that human activity, at a given time, will have consequences which influence future human activity; so that institutions, for the most part, develop independently of what is willed for them. Now we must be careful about drawing facile comparisons but there is, it seems to me, a real connection at this point between Marx's treatment of social institutions and Wittgenstein's treatment of mathematics and logic. We may say that what Wittgenstein tried to show was that there is not, in addition to natural fact and the activities of mathematicians, something called Mathematics, but that this does not mean that mathematical operations are arbitrary and can be altered at will.

portance. One may be perfectly intelligible in broken English
and entirely unintelligible though one's sentences are constructed perfectly.

Now what applies to language in general applies in particular
to developing a system in mathematics or in logic. As I have
said, to people who have a similar physiology, who share a
common training, and who confront a common world, certain
facts will suggest others and the people, even when they work
independently of one another, will agree in the way they
proceed. The mathematician or the logician develops his system
not by peering into the future but by looking for a pertinent
connection with what has gone before, being reasonably
confident that what strikes him as pertinent will strike others as
pertinent also. In this he is as much a creator as a discoverer; and
since, like the composer of a variation, he has only what has
gone before to rely on, he cannot guarantee that he will find the
pertinent connection he seeks, nor even that there is such a connection to be found.

In the light of this last remark, it will be useful to conclude by
considering what Wittgenstein has to say in his later work
about Russell's paradoxes. On Wittgenstein's later view, one
does not properly understand a paradox such as that of the Liar
until one has become puzzled about how anyone can be puzzled
by it. For it is very easy to give an account of how the paradox
arises, no step of which is in the least puzzling. For example,
consider the statement 'This is false'. It is evident that the truth
grounds of this proposition, in its most usual employment, are
parasitic on those of another. In other words, normally when
someone says 'This is false', he is referring to some other statement (say, 'It is raining'), and one does not know whether what
he says is itself true or false until one has determined the truth or
falsity of the other statement (it is raining). Thus if 'It is raining'
is false, the statement 'This is false' is true; if 'It is raining' is true,
the statement is false.

Now notice that if someone asks us to treat 'This is false' as referring to itself, he is asking us to extend the use of the sentence beyond its normal employment. There is, of course, no reason in itself why we should not do so. We have extended the use of a sentence beyond its normal employment when we treat 'This sentence contains five words' as referring to itself. In this case it seems fairly natural to do so; we have little difficulty, in short, in determining whether the sentence in its new use is true or false. Notice, however, that there is a vital difference between the two cases. A sentence of the form 'X contains five words' does not depend for its truth or falsity on the truth or falsity of some other sentence. The procedure normally used in verifying it can be applied just as easily to the sentence itself as to any other. But the truth or falsity of 'This is false' mainifestly does depend on the truth or falsity of some other sentence. In short, when we treat 'This is false' as referrring to itself, we are not simply extending its use, we are removing from its normal use one of the features essential to it. It is therefore not at all surprising that we should get into trouble. It would be very surprising if we did not.

But what this does not explain, it might be said, is the particular form the trouble takes. Why does it take the form of a paradox, a contradiction? This is very easily explained. The contradiction arises because, though we are no longer using the sentence normally, we continue to apply to it, by analogous reasoning, some of the features of its normal use. Thus, as we have said, the truth grounds of 'This is false' are so related to those of another statement that when the other statement is true, 'This is false' is false, and when false, it is true. Now by analogous reasoning, if 'This is false' refers to *itself* then if it is true (it is important not to look too closely at what that is supposed to mean) it is false, and if it is false, it is true. We have our contradiction.

Now it is essential not to react to this contradiction by attempting to explain it away. If we are correct in our account, this will in any case be impossible. For the whole point of the account is to show that the contradiction is only to be expected. What would be surprising, indeed miraculous, given the way we are using, or attempting to use, the sentence 'This is false', is that a contradiction should *not* arise. What we should consider is not the contradiction but the way people have reacted to it. Why, in short, have people attempted to explain it away, been puzzled by it?

The answer, it seems to me, is not far to seek. The contradiction will be puzzling only if one approaches it with a preconveived view, according to which it *cannot* be there. For example, if one holds that the development of a logical system reflects some underlying flawless structure then the appearance of the contradiction will seem explicable only on the assumption of some human error. It will appear, in short, as something to be explained away. But now it has been the burden of this chapter to show that such a view is misconceived. Following Wittgenstein, we have argued that a logical or mathematical system is a human construction in which, relying on a common sense of what is relevant or pertinent, we seek to build on what has gone before. Since we have nothing to rely on except what has gone before we cannot guarantee that in extending our system we shall be indefinitely successful. Now viewed from this angle, the contradiction we are considering will not seem at all puzzling. All it will prove is that we cannot hope to extend our procedures indefinitely without ever getting into trouble.

This point was indeed implicit in the first example we considered in the present chapter. We said that the use of ' $\sim p$ ' does not guarantee an unambiguous use to ' $\sim\sim p$ '. Some will find it pertinent to use the latter sign as equivalent to ' p '; others, as equivalent to $\sim p$. The facts do not assimilate themselves to our common sense of what is pertinent. But then the matter becomes undecidable;[2] we hit a snag. Wittgenstein's point is that the existence of such snags should not surprise us.

[2] I mean, of course, within the system. Obviously we can alter the system one way or another, say, on grounds of convenience.

The latter point is one that needs to be elaborated further, for Wittgenstein has been widely misunderstood in what he said about ambiguity and contradiction. For example, it has been said that, for Wittgenstein, a contradiction in mathematics does not matter at all. But this is a complete misunderstanding. Wittgenstein's point was that a contradiction in mathematics, or anywhere else, is harmful *only where it causes harm*. Obviously it is harmful if it holds us up or impedes communication. But it does not do this *merely* by existing. In other words, the existence of a contradiction within a system is neither surprising nor harmful in itself. We can easily illustrate this by referring to 'This is false'. As we have seen, if the use of the sentence is extended in a certain way we are landed with a contradiction. But the point is that the condition of the contradiction's arising is that the sentence is *not* used in the usual way, i.e., in the way that everyone will want to use it. For this reason, the contradiction, so far as ordinary language is concerned, is entirely harmless. Where people want to use the sentence, no contradiction exists; it only exists where no one would want to use the sentence. In other words, it is merely superstition to treat a contradiction as a kind of creeping poison which if it occurs in one part of a system will gradually seep through the system as a whole. Either a contradiction in a system causes harm or it does not; if it does not, we can ignore it; if it does, we can take steps to deal with it.

It will be seen, then, that Wittgenstein's treatment of Russell's paradox is in line with the whole of his later view of logic. In summary, his later view runs as follows. A logical or mathematical system is a human construction. It begins in an agreed use of signs. We can develop a system because the way we originally use the signs leads to their future use. One can say if one wishes that the earlier uses determine the later. But the determination is a matter of fact not of logic. It works through human and physical nature. *When* there is an agreement in the use of signs and in the development of that use, we have logical principles, for these merely register and crystallize the way we use signs. In other words, logical principles arise out of the use of language; they do not underlie it.

It is to be hoped that by contrast with this later view the earlier will stand out the more clearly.

THE CONTENTS OF THE TRACTATUS

The following analytical table of contents may prove useful to students who are already familiar with the main part of this book.

Facts 1–1.21

'The world is all that is the case.' The propositions that follow this are its elucidation. Thus 'all that is the case' is the totality of *facts*, not of things. The difference between 'facts' and 'things' is elucidated by the statement that it is the facts in *logical space* that are the world.

States of affairs 2–2.0141

'What is the case – a fact – is the existence of states of affairs.' The section beginning with this proposition is a further elucidation of the propositions falling under one. A fact is a state of affairs; it is something complex. The things that make up the complex appear in a certain combination; but they might have been combined differently. In logic, however, nothing is accidental. If a thing *can* occur in a state of affairs the possibility of the state of affairs msut be written into the thing itself. A speck in the visual field need not be red, but it must have some colour;

notes must have some pitch, objects of touch some degree of hardness, and so on. Objects exist in logical space, so that if I know an object I also know all its possible occurrences in states of affairs.

Objects 2.02–2.063

'Objects are simple.' A state of affairs is complex, so every statement about a state of affairs can be resolved into a statement about its constituents. But every statement about its constituents cannot itself be resolved into a further statement, otherwise there would be no contact between language and the world. At some point therefore words must just stand for objects, these objects being simple. Only when words stand for objects can something be said. Moreover whatever is said involves complexity, involves the combination of objects. To say that something is red, for example, is to represent a combination of objects, a state of affairs. (This is why an object in itself is, in a manner of speaking, colourless.) A combination of objects can be represented because it is possible for the objects so represented to appear in that combination. This is a matter of logic. What is the case, reality, the world depends on which among these possible states of affairs actually exist. This is a matter of fact. Logic determines only what is possible; it cannot determine what is the case.

Pictures 2.1–2.225

'We picture facts to ourselves.' A proposition pictures; it is the representation of a possible state of affairs, of what might be so. The elements of a proposition stand for objects; they are their representatives. These elements are related to one another in a determinate form. The form that the elements take constitutes the picturing. The fact that the elements of the picture are related in a determinate form *is* a representation of how things are in the world. So there must be something in common between the form of the proposition and the form of the objects it represents. But what the proposition pictures is a possible state of affairs; it cannot picture its own form. Moreover, whether or not it is true is a different question from what it pictures. In order to know whether it is true one must first know what it pictures and then compare it with reality. It will picture the same thing whether or not it is true.

Thought   3–3.13

'A logical picture of facts is a thought.' This can be read the other way round: a thought is a logical picture of facts. In other words a thought is a thought only when it has the logical structure of a proposition or picture. (But this interpretation is controversial. The student is advised to look at pages 30–3 of this book where the matter is discussed in detail.)

Proposition and name   3.14–3.261

'What constitutes a propositional sign is that in it its elements (the words) stand in a determinate relation to one another.' The sense of a proposition lies in its structure. In this it is to be contrasted with a name. A name does not possess pictorial form; it just stands for an object in the world, which is its meaning. But the meaning, or better, the sense of a proposition is not something for which it stands in the world. The sense of a proposition is not external to that proposition as the meaning of a name is external to that name. This is why a proposition has the same sense whether or not it is true, whether or not it corresponds to something in the world.

Logic and convention   3.262–3.5

'What signs fail to express, their application shows. What signs slur over, their application says clearly.' It is only because a proposition is a collection of signs having logical structure that it has a sense and it is only within such a structure that name has meaning. But logical structure is not always clearly revealed by signs. For example, one and the same sign, as written or spoken, may have different uses, as when the word 'is' figures sometimes as the copula, sometimes as a sign of identity, and sometimes as an expression for existence. Here the word 'is' really stands for three different symbols and this is evident in its application, in there being three quite different rules for its use. Thus logical form or structure is revealed not by the way signs look or sound, not by what is conventional, but by their *application*. In this way logic distinguishes itself from what is arbitrary or conventional. For although it is an arbitrary matter that the word 'is' should be used at all, it is not an arbitrary matter that certain things should follow when it is given one use and not when it is given another, that one can say some things when it is used as the copula but not when it is used as a sign of identity. The advantage of a formal notation or symbolism is that it makes that clear. In an adequate symbolism the difference in the application of signs would be marked by differences in the signs themselves, so that logical form would be adequately displayed. In this way what is essential to a proposition would be clearly distinguishable from what is conventional or arbitrary. (Propositions 3.33–3.333 concern Russell's theory of types. For a discussion of this, see pages 55–7 of this book.)

Philosophy   4–4.0031

'A thought is a proposition with a sense.' What does not have sense is not a proposition and cannot be thought. But, as we have seen, the sense of a proposition can be disguised; grammar, convention, can mislead one as to logical form. So misled, one may utter words which have only the appearance of constituting a proposition. Words may be uttered, in short, which have no clear application, no clear logic. Much of philosophy consists of such utterences. It springs from a failure to understand the logic of our language. Philosophy, properly understood, is therefore in a special way 'a critique of language'; it is a restoring of words to their proper sense.

True and false   4.01–4.0641

'A proposition is a picture of reality.' If I understand a proposition I know the situation it represents. To understand a proposition is to know what is the case if it is true and one can indicate the meaning of a proposition by indicating what would make it true as opposed to what would make it false. So a proposition's being either true or false is not a *consequence* of its having a meaning. Rather, to understand what would make it true and what false *is* to understand its meaning. It follows that the negation sign does not introduce a new discrimination of fact. If one understands a proposition one knows what would make it false and *so far as the facts are concerned* one has nothing further to grasp in order to understand the negation of that proposition. (See pages 38–9 for a further discussion.)

Philosophy and science   4.1–4.116

'Propositions represent the existence and non-existence of states of affairs.' The totality of true propositions constitutes the natural sciences. Philosophy is not one of the natural sciences. It is not a body of doctrine but an activity. Its task is the clarification of thought. So far as it takes itself to be a doctrine it is confused. It confuses what can be said with what can only be shown.

Formal concepts   4.12–4.2

'Propositions can represent the whole of reality, but they cannot represent what they must have in common with reality in order to be able to represent it – logical form.' Logical relations are formal properties. The attempt to state the formal properties of a concept is confused. These cannot be stated but show themselves in the application of the symbol. Thus to assert ' "It is raining" is a proposition', or 'Red is a colour' or 'One is a number' is nonsensical. 'It is raining', for example, shows that it is a proposition, that it is intelligible, in what it says. Nothing further is added in trying to state that it is. (Wittgenstein in this section introduces the important notion of a formal series. But see propositions 5.2–5.541 for a more detailed treatment.)

Truth function   4.21–4.45

'The simplest kind of proposition, an elementary proposition, asserts the existence of a state of affairs.' The propositions of ordinary language are complex; they are made up of elementary propositions. A complex proposition is a truth function of elementary propositions, i.e. the truth or falsity of the proposition as a whole will depend on the truth or falsity of its elementary constituents. The ways in which the truth or falsity of the proposition as a whole may be determined by the truth or falsity of its constituents can be set out in the form of a truth table. A truth table *is* a propositional sign. For example, the same propositional sign can be written either as '$p \vee q$' or as '$(TTTF)(p,q)$'.

Tautology   4.46–5.101

'Among the possible groups of truth-conditions there are two extreme cases.' We can construct propositions which are false whatever the truth possibilities of their constituent propositions and others which are true whatever these possibilities. We can construct contradictions and tautologies. Tautologies say nothing. One knows nothing about the weather if one knows that it is either raining or not raining. But tautologies are not nonsensical. They are part of the symbolism. Unlike gibberish, they show something about logical form. The propositions of logic are tautologies.

Inference   5.11–5.156

'If all the truth-grounds that are common to a number of propositions are at the same time truth-grounds of a certain proposition, then we say that the truth of that proposition follows from the truth of the others.' Logical inference rests entirely on the internal relations between propositions. If '*p*' follows from '*q*' in logic, they are themselves the only possible justification for the inference. The 'laws of inference' which are supposed to justify inference are superfluous. There is no hierarchy amongst the propositions of logic. All are on the same level and all say the same thing, namely, nothing. In developing a logical system one is merely elaborating the internal connections between propositions, showing how their senses are interrelated. (In this section and briefly in the last Wittgenstein discusses probability. See pages 80 and 81 of this book for a further discussion).

Formal operation   5.2–5.54

This is a complex section in which Wittgenstein's account of formal operations, the general form of the proposition, the significance of logical symbolism, and generality are intertwined. For an adequate account of the material the student is best advised to turn to chapters 4 and 6 of this book.

Wittgenstein has now largely completed his account of the proposition and of logic. In the remaining sections he is mainly concerned with those propositions which at first sight seem not to fit conveniently into his account. Often the discussion in these sections is too complex to admit of useful summary. Where this is so, I shall adopt the procedure I have adopted in the case of section 5.2–5.54. I shall indicate the topic and then refer to the chapter in this book in which it is discussed in detail.

Statements of belief 5.541–5.5423

The difficulty with '*A* believes that *p*' is that it seems not to be truth-functional. For a discussion of how Wittgenstein resolves the difficulty see chapter 8.

Logic, the world and the self 5.55–5.641

This section includes Wittgenstein's discussion of solipsism. See chapter 9. It is important for the student to note that Wittgenstein is not putting forward a version of solipsism; rather, he is giving solipsism as an example of a philosophical confusion which has arisen through not seeing the difference between what can be said and what can only be shown.

Logic and mathematics 6–6.241

What is important in this section is to see the precise way in which mathematics and logic are related. Mathematics is a method of logic. It is not derived from a set of logical principles. Rather, it is an aspect of the fundamental logical operation by which any proposition is derived from another. For a detailed discussion see chapter 5.

Natural science   6.3–6.372

Here Wittgenstein further elucidates the difference between the generality of logic and accidental generality by considering the nature of scientific laws. See chapter 7.

Value   6.373–6.522

An expression of value is not a statement of fact. All propositions are of equal value because all propositions merely say what is the case. But what is the case, what happens to be so, is not the same as what ought to be so, what is valuable. For a further discussion see chapter 10.

What can be said and what can only be shown   6.53–7

For a discussion of the complex issues raised by these last propositions see chapter 11.

INDEX